The Family Bank

The Family Bank

The Family Guide to Financially Successful Children

Sergio Dinaro

AuthorHouse™
1663 Liberty Drive
Bloomington, IN 47403
www.authorhouse.com
Phone: 1-800-839-8640

© 2012 by Sergio Dinaro. All rights reserved.

No part of this book may be reproduced, stored in a retrieval system, or transmitted by any means without the written permission of the author.

Published by AuthorHouse   06/27/2012

ISBN: 978-1-4772-2390-1 (sc)
ISBN: 978-1-4772-2391-8 (hc)
ISBN: 978-1-4772-2392-5 (e)

Library of Congress Control Number: 2012910812

Any people depicted in stock imagery provided by Thinkstock are models, and such images are being used for illustrative purposes only.
Certain stock imagery © Thinkstock.

This book is printed on acid-free paper.

Because of the dynamic nature of the Internet, any web addresses or links contained in this book may have changed since publication and may no longer be valid. The views expressed in this work are solely those of the author and do not necessarily reflect the views of the publisher, and the publisher hereby disclaims any responsibility for them.

Cover art and all illustrations by the very talented Heather Workman

This book is dedicated to:

my Mom, my chief editor

my wife Wafa, my chief supporter . . . / critic

my friends and family who helped me make sense of my ideas

my Grandmother . . . "see grandma, I learned this stuff eventually" . . .

and finally to my daughter, inspiration and "Guinea pig" Kaitlyn, you were a trooper Sweetie . . .

The Family Bank
The Family Guide to Financially Successful Children

Our Bank Members Never Fail ix

Section I: Opening The Family Bank 1
    Chapter 1 The CEO and the Mentor (and the Parent):
        Understanding the Mindset 3
    Chapter 2 The CEO 6
    Chapter 3 The Mentor 11
    Chapter 4 The Parent: Retaining your Identity 22
    Chapter 5 Setting up The Family Bank 26

Section II: Moving and Controlling Money 47
    Chapter 6 Savings Account 53
    Chapter 7 Checking Account 59
    Chapter 8 Automatic Teller Machines (ATM) 63

Section III: Family Bank Employment 67
    Chapter 9 Searching for Employment 71
    Chapter 10 Building a Resume 85
    Chapter 11 Preparing for the Interview 96
    Chapter 12 The Interview 110
    Chapter 13 The Callback 115

Section IV: Professional Development..117
    Chapter 14 Rules of the Daily Grind..........................121
    Chapter 15 Vacation and Sick Time 127
    Chapter 16 Write-ups..131
    Chapter 17 Termination...136
    Chapter 18 Bonuses and Raises 142
Section IV: Paying Bills 145
    Chapter 19 Lunch Money..149
    Chapter 20 Rent 151
Section V: Managing Money..153
    Chapter 21 Credit and Your Credit Score....................159
    Chapter 22 Interest 173
    Chapter 23 Credit Cards..178
    Chapter 24 Loans..190
Section VII: Entrepreneurship...199
    Chapter 25 Starting Up the Family Bank
                  Small Business..203
    Chapter 26 Creating the Business Proposal 206
    Chapter 27 Presenting the Business Proposal................212
    Chapter 28 Running The Family Business....................219
Section VIII: Life Long Financial Success 221

Our Bank Members Never Fail

What is The Family Bank?

Simply put, The Family Bank is a how-to guide on how to create a bank in your home, in which you are the CEO and your children are your customers. This book is the guide to develop and implement this easy-to-use financial system that teaches your children everything they need to know about how adults control, manage, earn, spend, invest and ultimately lose their money. This system is called The Family Bank and Financial System. The Family Bank is only part of the Family Financial System, so I'll refer to The Family Bank when I'm discussing money management and I'll refer to the Family Financial System for more extended topics, such as resume writing and applying for Family Bank Employment . . . oh yes, we are much more than just a bank.

Mastering money and finances at a young age is a completely foreign concept in our culture, but it will give your children the twelve years of financial experience that you and I didn't have until we were 30! Imagine how your life might be different if you knew the long-term benefits of money management at age eighteen that you know now.

The Family Bank, like a hammer, is a tool. It's a vital tool in your tool belt that will reduce the amount of time and energy it takes to build for your children the foundation of one of the most important lessons they need to learn, which is how to control and manage their money. You might be skeptical because, let's face it, you probably don't love hammers. After all, they look like, feel like and generally represent work, but have you ever tried to build a house without one? It's possible, but I wouldn't recommend it. Teaching your children how to build a strong financial future without using The Family Bank might also be possible, but again, why work that hard without tools when it's no longer necessary?

Understanding The Family Bank is simple, and implementing it takes minimal effort, but utilizing it enthusiastically will reap unbelievable dividends for both you and your children; so in your hands you have a powerful tool. The Family Bank gives you the framework to teach your children everything they need to know, which happens to be everything you already know, about how to make money, control money and how to make money work *for* your children, instead of against them.

How did I end up here? Life without The Family Bank . . .

If you're anything like me, then at some point in your life you've stopped and asked yourself: How did I end up here? . . . and realized that it all seems a little bit hazy. Yet, here we sit; a home, kids, bills and responsibilities that won't give us a minute of peace. As I head blindly through this chapter of my life, I find myself spending a substantial amount of time looking back at the decisions I've made that led me here. Life is dramatic and complicated, but I have noticed that each period of my life seems to have a theme to it: from the deep, pure emotionalism of adolescence to the impulsive idealism of young adulthood; from the wonder and excitement of entering the workforce, to finishing school and the crushing pressure and stress of today. Am I alone here? I bet I'm not. Don't get me wrong, I love where I'm at in my life, but how the heck did I get here? And why do I never have the money to do both what I need to do and what I want to do? Is it this way for everyone? . . . No, not everyone struggles with finances, but that isn't very comforting is it? Well, if it helps, most of us *are* struggling.

Fifteen years ago I really thought that old people like "present day me" would have everything in order by now. Back then my parents would tell me that their goal in life was to make sure that my life turns out a little better than theirs did. But what constitutes better? If I'm lying awake at night trying to figure out how to pay my mortgage, then compared to my parents who were lying in bed awake at night trying to figure out how to pay the rent, am I really any better off? Am I happier? Do I have any less stress? Everybody wants their children to have a better life than they did, but are we really giving our kids the tools they need to be truly successful? No, we're not.

We're so focused on putting food on the table that we're forced to tell ourselves our kids will have a better life than we do now, because we give them a nice home and help them with their homework. We want to give our kids the world and every opportunity in it, but at this point we may need a miracle to get to where we'd like to be financially; and miracles don't happen to people like us . . . or do they?

Yes, they do. The way our children blindly adore us, internalize every word, every expression, and every lesson we teach them *is* a miracle. When you try to teach something, anything really, to an adult, they are usually too full of their own biases and preconceived ideas to listen, but your children learn from you without hesitation and without reservation . . . whether we like it or not. Your children soak up every lesson, regardless of its value.

So, how will the miracle of children help you pay the bills? It won't, but then again, this book isn't for you, is it? It is about using your God-given ability to impart wisdom and knowledge to your kids, to teach them the lessons about money, employment, credit, interest and business etiquette that you wish you could have learned while growing up. The Family Bank is about how to give your kids a better life than you have now, by teaching them how to not just survive in modern society, but to thrive.

Can The Family Bank really give your children a better life?

Children are highly impressionable and our children's minds, personalities and values are easily malleable by lessons taught early in life, and no one has more influence over how your children turn out than you do. We don't remain malleable forever, though; around eighteen years old our ideals solidify and it becomes increasingly difficult to change the habits we've developed, regardless of their value. This is why it is so important to teach our children early how our financial system works; to let them use it, touch it, make mistakes with it, in order to to make sense of it and to see how they fit into it.

"Oh, to know then what you know now!" We can't change the past, but we *can* mold our children's futures, so now it's time to imbue them with the knowledge we wish we had been given back when it would have done us some good. You have wisdom, experience and an attentive audience; what you don't have is *spare time!* This book won't teach you anything you don't already know; however, it does all the work of organizing every painful lesson you've learned during your life into an elegantly simple plan that you can implement with **minimal** time and energy. Why wrap up all your experience into an easy to use system to teach your children everything you know about finances and surviving in the real world? Because no one else will, and so you can teach your kids how *not* to make financial mistakes later in life; and more importantly, how to make the limited amount of money they earn work *for* them.

Teaching your children everything they need to know about the real world financial system might seem too daunting a task for any parent. Enter . . . The Family Bank. Creating your own Family Bank, using this book as your guide, simplifies and streamlines a painfully complicated task. By implementing The Family Bank in your home you will be able to teach your children everything they need to know about finances in the real world, with a minimum amount of time and energy required. Sound too good to be true? It's not. The hardest part of teaching lessons to children is making the lessons tangible and understandable. To create your own system like The Family Bank from the ground up would take years to perfect, trust me! But the hard part has been done for you, so just sit back, relax and follow the step by step model put forth in this book. With only one Weekly Meeting and five minutes here and there to update your records, your children will become responsible, independent financial gurus by the time they turn eighteen years old. Best of all, it's easy.

Is The Family Bank really necessary?

The financial system in our evolving world is complex; but, for better or for worse, it's not difficult to use. In fact, swiping a credit card is so easy that most people get into credit debt without understanding the long-term effects of their credit card's compounding interest. Our society gives us the tools to turn the poorest hard worker into a millionaire, but it does so by setting the majority of us up for failure. The handful that become financially independent do so because most of us give them all our money . . . actually we give them a lot *more* than all our money! What do the successful have that the rest of don't? A Harvard education? Actually, no; what they have is an understanding of how to make our financial system work for them.

School and a good education are imperative to success in life; no one denies that, but inevitably that is not what makes people financially responsible or financially successful. We've all heard stories of people who started out poor and ended up rich; sometimes they had an education and sometimes they became wealthy without a college degree. We've also heard stories of famous people who have made millions of dollars, but still ended up broke, in the end. Education is important, but unless your kids specifically study Finance in college, it's not going to help them manage and retain their money. A college education will definitely increase your child's earning potential. However, like the mistakes that will be made by so many of his peers, it won't teach him how to retain and grow that money.

Instead of college, other people focus on developing natural talent for earning tons of money, which is great; but again it's not going to teach your kids how to hold on to that money. So, if a formal education is not the magic bullet and amazing talent is also not it, then what is *it*? It is learning the value of money, how money works and how money can work for or against them; learning it early enough in life to take advantage of this knowledge is the real key to maintaining wealth. And guess who is the only person who can teach this vital lesson to your kids? If you said the public school system, then slap yourself! No, of course it's not school; it's you and only you.

Understanding and utilizing the modern financial system at an early age is the cornerstone to being financially successful as an adult. Basically, your kids need to understand early in life how to make a little pile of money and how to make it grow over time, instead of making a little financial hole and making *it* grow over time. It's starting to sound like common sense, right? Obviously then, schools must spend a great deal of time teaching our kids about credit cards, checking accounts, interest, writing a resume, and applying for jobs . . . except that they don't! It seems that the modern public education system has completely missed the most important lesson to financial success as an adult, which is how to function in the modern financial world.

Being exactly where you want to be financially is something that eludes most people. Sadly, parents either don't realize they need to teach their kids about the modern financial system, or they don't know how to simplify it into something that children can grasp. After all, our financial system is so complicated and our kids are just *so* innocent.

Now, people aren't dumb and I know that parents aren't lazy, so there has to be a reason that every family hasn't already implemented a comprehensive educational family program on fiscal responsibility. On the surface it seems like a lot of work and, truthfully, it seems a little unnatural to burden children with that which stresses us out so much . . .

"financial responsibility". So, why does it seem unnatural to teach children about the real world? Is it because it's what we as adults think of as the "adult burden", which we carry around on our shoulders like Atlas carrying the weight of the world? It almost seems like we don't want to stress our kids out with the pressure of being grown-ups. Those "adult" financial responsibilities are what we shield our children from specifically because it causes us so much stress. Parents aren't neglectful; they are just protecting their kids from the adult burden of stress, right?

No. I mean, let's be realistic. Does shielding our children really protect them from the stress of financial hardship? Look at the average person's debt in this country and then think about the path your children are heading down. Protecting our kids from learning adult fiscal responsibility is not working. Is it really worth it to shield them from ten years of a little work just to crush them with debt and stress for the next seventy years? No, it's not worth it. By inoculating your children with a little knowledge, a little work, and yes, a taste of the stress of making small financial decisions, you will immunize them from a lifetime of the stress of playing financial catch-up.

The Family Bank teaches children all the basics of the financial system without inflicting all the real world damage and stress, and it accomplishes this task because *you* play the role of the "real world". Your children know with absolute certainty that you love and care for them and that you (as The Family Bank) will always do what is best for them. Sound familiar? No, probably not. That element of love and nurturing is what you and I don't get from "real world" banks and creditors. When we don't pay our bills the credit companies beat us down, which causes us tremendous stress. The Family Bank is successful because it is founded in love and trust, and backed by you, who would never let your members fail.

Are you now wondering how your kids are going to learn about the real world if you take all the stress and scariness out of it? It's simple: first, it doesn't matter because you're teaching them the mechanics of the system, not the feeling they get from it; second, they will, in fact, learn how to cope with the little stresses they face when making financial decisions on their own. Decisions like whether or not your son should apply for a loan from The Family Bank to buy Mom a birthday present, if he knows he doesn't currently have the income to pay it back? That is where your creativity, intuition and experience (and a few pointers from The Family Bank) turn this book into a real, functional, educational system. For example, if you know your son can't pay back a loan for birthday presents, then you'll still give him the loan and let him default on it. The Family Bank will teach him the real life consequences of making poor financial decisions, by repossessing the game console that he put up as collateral, and dropping his Family Bank Credit Score. But we don't stop there; then, you'll take the time to sit with him and teach him how to rebuild that credit score and how to make the money he needs to repurchase his lost game console. Many lessons are tough, but you'll always be there to soften those tough blows and turn them into teaching points. On a lighter note, many lessons are just fun, and then you'll just relax and have fun with it. We'll get into more details later, though.

In the end, the quality time spent with you, in conjunction with the self-confidence your children will develop in their ability to understand and use the modern financial system for their own benefit, will massively outweigh the work you and your children put into running and using the Family Bank. The Family Bank always teaches positive lessons, develops valuable skills and builds knowledge and self-confidence in your young bank members, preparing them for the real world that lies ahead.

So, we've covered the fact that financial success has very little to do with how much money we make. Rather, it's about how long it takes us to learn to navigate the financial system and to recover from the inevitable mistakes we make when we're young, which usually stem from credit and interest mishaps. We also discussed that these lessons are not usually covered in school. Learning the financial system is an education gap that we, as responsible and loving parents, are thus required to fill. Now, I challenge you with these rhetorical questions: are you qualified to teach something of this magnitude to your kids? and, if so, when should you start?

To these questions, I give the following example as an answer. Everyone has a natural love of something right from the very beginning of life: sports, art, music, reading, science, dancing, or anything else. For me, it was football. What was *your* first love? Did you end up reaching your full potential in that field? I didn't. You know what would have helped me? If my Dad had been a professional football player who started playing football with me and teaching me football skills from the time I was able to hold a ball, and continued to teach me more and more every day of my life while I was growing up. Having a professional mentor would have helped me go much farther in my otherwise short-lived football career. Wouldn't you like to have had a professional (fill in the blank with whatever your passion was) as a parent, who dedicated his life to teaching you his talent? Well, guess what? You are a professional Adult. You work, you manage your family finances on a daily basis, you have finely developed skills that you acquired as an Adult, and no one else is more qualified to teach your kids how to be a responsible Adult than you are. So when should you get started? The sooner the better.

Malcolm Gladwell, in his book *Outliers,* discusses the necessity of obtaining 10,000 hours of focused practice at a task in order to become an expert at that task, whatever it may be. In a nutshell, the purpose of the The Family Bank is to do just that; to give your children the requisite experience using our modern financial system to become experts at running their own personal finances **before** they get thrown out onto the harsh and unforgiving financial world at age eighteen.

As I've already stated, everything I explain in this book you already know. You know it because you've lived it. You've already learned every lesson in this book and you've already had the unfortunate pleasure of learning it the hard way. Actually, the hardest way possible, by making mistake after mistake, which if you're anything like me, set you back financially about fifteen years. As a parent, we all want to make our children's lives better than ours are now. We teach our children how to love, how to laugh and if we're really good, the difference between right and wrong. These are essential qualities that we work hard at teaching, but somehow, as a society, we have a tendency to overlook teaching our kids about how to function financially as adults. We miss it, the school system misses it, everyone misses it. This begs the question: why does everyone overlook these vitally important lessons? It's something we all know (learned the hard way, of course) and yet, we don't pass it along to our kids.

Maybe we justify not teaching our children about money management, the pitfalls of interest, and how to function in the professional world, by thinking that because we learned it through the school of hard knocks, our kids should, too; after all, it builds character and a respect for money, right? That idea would be great, except that it's completely false. Let's be honest, if you knew "then" what you know "now", wouldn't you have done things differently? Yes, you would have, we all would have. Have you ever dreamed about having a time machine? One where you could go back in time, even if just for long enough to teach yourself some significant financial lessons that you could have used to prevent having made some of those less than beneficial financial decisions? Well, actually, you do, and she's right in front of you. Your kids are smaller, younger, better looking, smarter versions of yourself just waiting for you to teach them all the hard lessons you have already struggled through. So let's get started . . .

SECTION I

Opening The Family Bank

Chapter 1

The CEO and the Mentor (and the Parent): Understanding the Mindset

Both the CEO and the Mentor are literal positions in The Family Bank. Everything you do teaches your kids lessons about life, but in this case you have actual roles in The Family Bank as a Mentor and a CEO, in order to teach your children specific lessons about money and about the financial world. Let's take a look.

Congratulations! You've just been promoted to Corporate Executive Officer (CEO) of the most important business organization in the world: The (insert your family name here) Family Bank! Unlike Wall Street, The Family Bank's worth is determined by the "values" gained by your children, as they are your primary investment. Thus, being the CEO is important, but your #1 priority is to be an individual Mentor to each of your children. No two bank customer's needs are the same, and neither are the needs of each of your children. Each of your bank's members will have his own individual strengths and weaknesses, talents and needs; therefore, your job is to identify these needs and be a Mentor to each of your kids. We'll discuss how to do this in a minute, but first a word about how to not lose your identity as a parent while playing the roles of Mentor and of CEO.

It's important to explain up front that you will play the role of both the CEO and the Mentor (and also the Parent), but never at the same time. The Parent is not a specific role in The Family Bank; you will just work the roles of CEO and Mentor around being your child's parent.

The CEO runs The Family Bank, but the Mentor teaches your children how the bank works, how the financial system works and all the intricacies of finance. The CEO does not teach your children lessons, just like the CEO of any corporation is not going to sit you down and teach you how to not lose your money to his company. So, you are never going to "mentor" your child as the CEO; however, keep in mind that you are still always her parent. As a parent you create rules for your children that apply and are enforced at all times. Incorporating your roles as the CEO or as the Mentor will never trump your role as a parent. In fact, they will compliment it. The roles of CEO and of the Mentor are creations that enhance your power and ability to teach lasting and important lessons.

As a parent you set rules for your children, such as, "No buying candy without parental permission first." So, when you and your daughter are at the grocery store and your daughter decides to test the boundaries of the Family Bank by purchasing candy with her Family Bank Account, without your permission, what can you do?

Real banks don't stop you from making bad financial decisions, so you won't stop your daughter from spending her money, either. You will allow her to buy the candy without complaint and give her a receipt for her purchase (as the CEO). After she has purchased the candy, you will immediately confiscate it, because it is contraband and you did not give her permission to buy it (as the Parent). You will then take quick notes in your day planner of the details of the transaction and your thoughts on the matter, so that you can discuss her financial decision making process with her at your next Weekly Meeting (as the Mentor), which we will discuss in Chapter 3.

Now, if you're anything like me, the idea of not regulating your child's purchases on the spot is probably giving you pause right about now. Fear not! Chapter 4 will discuss this apparent dilemma thoroughly, and fully explain the reasons behind allowing your child to make her own financial decisions and mistakes.

So you see, each role in The Family Bank is distinct and separate, but they all work together in harmony around you being her parent, to successfully teach all the valuable lessons The Family Bank has to offer.

Chapter 2

The CEO

The CEO is a literal position. When you are running The Family Bank and Financial System you are the CEO of a major company. You manage money and you receive a service for the paychecks you give out. You also make money on interest from your clients. It's important to think of yourself as a CEO and to keep track of what your business is worth. You want to be able to post your profits, so that your bank members can see exactly how much of their hard earned money they are losing to you in interest.

You will play the role of the CEO at all times, except during the Weekly Meetings. The Weekly Meetings are the only time you play the role of the Mentor. The technical aspects of your position as CEO are simple; you run every aspect of The Bank. When you and your daughter are at the store and she wants to buy something, you will facilitate the transaction. (We'll cover how each type of transaction works in its respective section: for example, credit card transactions are in the Credit Card chapter.) When your son wants to apply for a loan at The Family Bank, he will come to see you, the CEO of The Family

Bank, at The (your last name) Family Bank and fill out an application. Basically, as the CEO, you handle all of the technical transactions regarding The Family Bank.

Moderation—

So far, we have discussed that The Family Bank is a teaching tool. Within The Family Bank you will teach your children the financial lessons they need to learn by using the roles of the Mentor and the CEO. Without getting into economic theory, your theme of mentoring will be along the lines of "moderation and calculated risk"; whereas, as the CEO, you are a business professional, teaching your children how to be business professionals. As the Mentor you will directly teach your children financial lessons, but as the CEO you will indirectly teach your children how the real world works. Teaching children about moderation is a complicated task, which requires both a Mentor to guide your child, and a CEO to emulate the real world.

Little Mr. Reckless needs you to guide him to create a manageable budget, whereas Little Miss Thrifty needs to learn that it's important to fulfill her "social obligations", such as buying birthday presents, even if it means she has to work a little overtime to pay back a small loan. Credit is an enormous part of our economic system, and learning how to use it can't be ignored in The Family Bank. Therefore, as the CEO, you will often find yourself in a position where you can explain the benefits of credit to your daughter. But keep in mind that when she is applying for a loan, you will only be pointing out the positive aspects of credit. As the Mentor, you will explain to your son the concept of credit and how it can help him and how it can hurt him; but as the

CEO, you will explain the "terms and conditions" of said credit when your son is sitting down in front of you in your office and filling out an application. As the CEO, you will both run your Family Bank and give your children the technical knowledge they need to properly use and understand the tools of The Family Bank.

Inevitably the topic of credit brings us to a point of contention. We will cover how to use credit in The Family Bank in depth later, but for now we need to discuss its relevance to The Family Bank and Financial System. After all, utilizing credit and charging interest is how you will make money as the CEO. Some people believe that you "NEVER buy anything you don't have the money for right now", whereas some people believe that "I breathe, therefore I swipe plastic". Most of you are somewhere in between those extremes. If I tried to go into detail about which philosophy is better here, I would make most of you mad and I'd waste hundreds of pages trying to defend myself. So, regardless of your personal views, my point here is simply that the purpose of The Family Bank is to teach your children *how* the system works. The only way to teach them how it works is to talk to them about it and then let them use it.

I understand if you believe that credit is evil and I understand if you never want your kids to ever take out a loan for anything, but if you decide to cut out the credit portion in order to shield them from making loans with The Family Bank, then all you are doing is creating a huge hole in your child's knowledge and understanding of the real world. A hole that they will inevitably fall into face first at age eighteen, which is the opposite of the outcome we are aiming for. Cutting out or controlling your children's ability to obtain and use credit would also make you a terrible CEO! So, I strongly encourage you to create your bank as realistically as possible and let your kids make the mistake of getting into debt over their heads while they are still with you. Let your inner CEO run wild! Let them learn the hard lessons while their credit scores still aren't real. Let them feel what it's like to get everything they want for a day and then work their little butts off for a year to try and pay it back; only to miss a payment, have their collateral repossessed and have to work for another year to rebuild their credit.

Sound harsh? I promise you, your kids won't even blink at their dropping credit scores (at first). In fact, the responsibility of being CEO of The Family Bank will stress you out infinitely more than it will stress out your kids. Be forewarned, though, this would all be for nothing if your kids didn't encounter hard times sooner or later. Those times will likely come when their credit has been shot for a year and they haven't shown the slightest bit of care about it, or until they can't buy any presents for their family or friends at Christmas, Eid, Hanukkah, or whichever holidays you observe. Then they'll begin the process of understanding the importance of moderation and fiscal responsibility.

I have not been trying to pick on the thrifty here, by spending so much time convincing you to utilize credit in The Family Bank. I'm just trying to get the point across that your Family Bank is a full financial system and the basics included in this book are the minimum skills required for your kids to be successful in the real world. How they implement these skills is still largely up to you. The bottom line here is that you are the CEO of The Family Bank, and CEO's want to (and live for) making money. So make money! When your kids use the bank, let them use all of it. Your bank is modeled after a real bank for a reason. As painful as it might be to let them make financial mistakes, remember, they have to make those mistakes in order to learn from them.

Chapter 3

The Mentor

As the Mentor, you will need to observe each child's behavior and general attitude toward money, and keep a journal of your observations. At the end of each week you will have a Weekly Meeting where you will sit down with each child individually and go over all the financial transactions he made that week, discuss any questions he has about anything you have taught him and teach him any new lessons you want him to learn that week. I will discuss the Weekly Meeting in detail in the next section.

Record keeping is extremely important in both your roles as CEO and as Mentor. Keep a journal (more details about your journal later) of every transaction for each bank member, but also take notes in your journal about the types of decisions that your kids struggle with and how they resolve those struggles. For example, let's take Christmas, or any holiday you observe, that maintains the social obligation of the giving of gifts. In this story you have two children, each of whom have not saved enough money this year to buy presents for their family members. The oldest, let's call her Miss Thrifty, might not want to take out loans from The Family Bank to buy presents, because she doesn't want to face the interest charges. You note that Miss Thrifty follows the mantra, "don't spend money I don't have". On the other hand you note that your youngest, let's call him Mr. Reckless, has no qualms about going into massive debt to buy everyone everything they want this year. Mr. Reckless' mantra is, "as long as the bank will lend it to me, then it's okay for me to take it; after all, they're the bank and they wouldn't give me money they thought I couldn't pay back". So, you will keep notes about the financial decisions your kids make and how they come to these decisions.

Different people naturally handle money in different ways, and keep in mind that days after your daughter completes a financial transaction you won't be able to remember all the details, so get used to writing everything down. This is why your notes are so incredibly important; your notes will be your guide during your Weekly Meetings. Also, by the time your kids graduate from high school you should have at least ten years' worth of transactions and financial decisions the two of you will sit down and analyze, reminisce over and probably laugh until you cry. I'll go into greater detail later, with suggestions on how to handle different scenarios as a Mentor, but for now it's important just to understand that each child is different and that you must take good notes and mentor each child individually, based on his or her unique needs. You are a Mentor and each child is a unique customer.

The Weekly Meeting—

The recording of your journal, whether electronically or the old fashioned way, is so that you can review your notes before your scheduled Weekly Meeting, which will last approximately 30 minutes;

let's say Saturday morning from 8am to 8:30am, or anytime during the week that is convenient for both you and your child.

Is a Weekly Meeting really necessary? Yes, the Weekly Meeting is absolutely imperative! If you can't commit to a Weekly Meeting then stop reading and put this book down right now . . . are you still here? . . . good. Okay, so we're agreed that you are committed to your children and, therefore, to the Weekly Meeting. Great, now I'm not joking here, I want you stop reading for a moment, hold this book or e-reader out in front of you and shake it up and down three times . . . go ahead . . . I'll wait. Okay, good, we shook on it; so you are now committed to a Weekly Meeting with each of your kids for somewhere around thirty minutes . . . each . . . individually.

Although you are the CEO of your bank, you are also a Mentor. I continue to make this distinction because it's important that these roles are understood, by all parties involved, to be completely separate roles. You are both, but never both at the same time. When you are the CEO you are not the Mentor, and conversely, when you are the Mentor, you are not the CEO. This will be hard to do at first, but in the end you don't want your children (through transference) believing that outside corporations will pull them aside and give them good "parental" advice. The job of the CEO, or of any business, is to get you to part with and lose your hard-earned money. The "good guys" are the good guys and the "bad guys" are the bad guys; your children have to learn that the bad guys are never the good guys and conversely, the good guys are never the bad guys! So, during your Weekly "Mentor" Meeting is when you will teach your children the financial lessons they need to learn. At all other times, you will be the CEO, which means you will facilitate financial transactions for you children, such as purchasing an item from a store.

The purpose of these Weekly Meetings is to give focus and direction to your children's educational needs. Although The Family Bank, once established, takes almost no effort to run, your kids can still only get out of it what you put into it. You'll have to spend a little time during the week, at your convenience, thinking about, planning and preparing for your weekly counseling sessions. Your preparation time really only needs to be a few minutes, to figure out what topic you will teach that week. After all, you're already an expert in these matters, so figure out what you want to talk about ahead of time and then just let it flow during your Weekly Meeting.

You're already an expert and you're their Mentor; you just have to focus those superpowers each week. Having said that, The Family Bank and Financial System is also a long-term project, so it's not necessary to cause yourself any more stress than you already have in your day trying to figure out what you're going to teach any one particular week. Some weeks you'll wing it and other weeks you will be genuinely inspired without even trying. As long as you are having a Weekly Meeting you are using The Family Bank correctly; and remember, The Family Bank is not a game, but it is meant to be fun!

One more note on preparation. Your preparation time is your own time, so enjoy it. Think about your kids, what you've taught them up to this point, what they're learning in school that might compliment what you are doing and what lessons you would like to see them start learning. You will automatically identify both the areas where they struggle and the areas where they excel. Take notes during this time and create an outline for your meeting. Some weeks you won't spend more than two minutes preparing, and some weeks, when you're genuinely inspired and have the time, you'll be likely to spend hours preparing. It all balances out in the end. Your forethought and organization during your meetings will instill trust and confidence in your kids, so try to never forget the prep! If this is sounding like too much work already, then think about the importance of your child's future and financial well-being. After all, we're only talking about spending 35 minutes a week with your child, here.

The Weekly Meeting in Action-

The Weekly Meeting is the heart of The Family Bank, because this is the time when you will teach your kids the lessons they need to know in order to be successful in life. The rest of The Family Bank is just implementing what they're learning and practicing it. One week, you will explain what a checking account is and how it works, one week you will be teaching her how to write a resume, or how to dress for an interview, and so on. Your Weekly Meetings are time set aside for you to teach your children all the lessons you had to learn the hard way. The Weekly Meeting is your time to teach your children everything you know about how to survive and thrive as an adult in modern society, and The Family Bank will give you a clear and thorough outline for what lessons you will need to teach during your Weekly Meetings.

Weekly Meetings are also versatile. Even though most of your Weekly Meetings will be the conventional "in your office meeting", some Weekly Meetings will be more like field trips. For example, you'll eventually schedule "business meetings" at a local restaurant to practice business dinner etiquette, or to let him close his new business deal with you. Sometimes you'll just take your daughter out for ice cream and show her what a real ATM looks like and how it works. The Weekly Meeting is the backbone of The Family Bank and Financial System and it is the time set aside for you to impart your wisdom onto your next generation, in whatever manner works best for the lesson you are trying to teach.

A couple of rules:

First, if one week you can't make your usual time, then you'll have to reschedule the Weekly Meeting to be at your daughter's earliest convenience, and the rescheduling can either be done in person or by phone. If your daughter is the one who reschedules the Weekly Meeting by phone, then this can be your opportunity to teach her phone etiquette. Learning how to make business calls is an important part of being successful as an adult. If your daughter wants to spend the night at a friend's house one weekend, then let her reschedule the meeting for later that weekend. When your son or daughter calls you to reschedule the Weekly Meeting, make sure you have taught them to be polite, non-argumentative and to ask you, "When are you free to reschedule the Weekly Meeting?" If they are calling to reschedule, then they have to work around your schedule, but that goes both ways. If you are the one who has to reschedule, then you must lead by example and ask them, "When are you free to have the Weekly Meeting?"

Side note: during the Weekly Meeting you are playing the role of the Mentor and your kids will call you Mom, not Ms. (your last name).

Your mentoring time is personal and it's your time to teach your kids one-on-one, Mother to daughter. The Family Bank is a business and so it's important to teach your children how to interact with business associates in a professional manner, even if their co-workers are also their friends. Simply put, mentoring time is personal time; all other interactions regarding The Family Bank are business time (even a phone call to reschedule a Weekly Meeting).

Second rule, no matter how many kids you have, it is mandatory that both business meetings and mentoring sessions are one-on-one. You've never gone into a bank and sat at a loan officer's desk at the same time as another random customer, while you both simultaneously talked about your own individual business. So don't make your kids do that. Meetings are one-on-one and mentoring time is one-on-one. It's the only way to address the individual needs of each of your children. Let's look back at the Christmas example from earlier in the book, when Mr. Reckless and Miss Thrifty were debating whether or not to obtain a Family Bank loan in order to buy presents. If you were to bring both your kids into the same Weekly Meeting and explain to Miss Thrifty that with a solid budget and good planning, a loan will help her to acquire the things she needs in life, such as a car and a house, while simultaneously explaining to Mr. Reckless that by taking out too many loans he will overextend himself, such as buying too big a car or house . . . well, you can see where this is going, and that your children will see this as you sending them mixed messages, and they will get confused. Just remember that your kids are young and the world still seems black and white to them, so your message at any given time needs to be equally clear and simple. Miss Thrifty: budget *and* fulfill your social obligations. Mr. Reckless: Budget, *then* fulfill your social obligations. In both situations you are teaching the same lesson: budget + fulfill social obligations = fiscal responsibility. Your kids are each unique, so you will need to allot time to mentor each of them individually.

An important note here about the "theme" of the Weekly Meeting: the mission of The Family Bank itself is not to teach liberal or conservative financial theory, as those lessons cannot possibly make sense to an eight year old, especially before she has even learned the mechanics of our financial system. The Family Bank is a system through which you are teaching your children how the modern financial system works in our country and how to successfully operate within it. When your child is older, say around sixteen to eighteen years old, and he has mastered the basics of our financial system, only then is it possible to begin incorporating your own personal financial ideology into your Weekly Meetings.

Everyone has their own views regarding spending, saving and investing, which people love to label as either liberal or conservative. Which one are you and how do you want your kids to be? Who cares? That's not what this book is about. This book is about teaching your kids how the system works, not about teaching theory. In fact, trying to teach financial theory to your children too early will only undermine The Family Bank and, inevitably, your own goal. For example, let's say your twelve-year-old decides she wants to go on a shopping spree at the mall and max out her credit cards. You won't be able intervene at the mall as the CEO, because that wouldn't make any sense; as the CEO you want her to use the tools of the Family Bank, especially her credit cards. In order to talk to her about her spending habits you'll wait until your next Weekly Meeting where you'll explain *that* the shopping spree was a bad idea, not *why* it was a bad idea. You will talk only about the actual damage done to her account, and not about the theoretical ideas of keeping a certain amount of money in her savings account at all times as a buffer. Later on, when your daughter is older, especially if she brings up the topic with you, you will teach her those theoretical lessons. However, in the beginning you want her to struggle with her accounts and her bills, and let her make up her own mind about how easy it is to get into debt "over her head".

Trust that your son will learn the consequences of dealing with loads of debt the hard way, through The Family Bank, and save the philosophical discussions for later, when they will mean something to him. Remember, as CEO you will always support your son's usage of checks, his debit card and his credit cards to shop. Don't slip into Mentor at the mall! Don't take a "time out" at the mall to give a Mentor "side note". Your Weekly Meeting is your only Mentoring time, while all other time is Family Bank CEO time. After your kids get older and have mastered the basics of The Family Bank, then you can take time during Weekly Meetings to discuss your views on fiscal responsibility; but make sure your children have mastered the principles of The Family Bank first. The lessons they learn on their own will inevitably "stick" much better anyway.

I've given it to you straight (not left or right) and here is why . . . now I'll tie this all together. The Family Bank is built on the foundation that we learn from experience. The Family Bank is hands-on, tangible and developed as a learning tool that has to be used and handled in order to be appreciated. Kids have to have the opportunity to make mistakes and to learn from them. Actually, that last line was so important that it's worth repeating again right here: *kids have to have the opportunity to make mistakes and to learn from them.* If you control what your children are allowed to spend their money on, and when, or use Weekly Meetings to stave off all the mistakes before they happen, and then say, "Look! See how nice your checking account looks!" it will make you feel good, but your kids won't learn a single thing about how to be financially responsible. You might think that the "on the spot" setting of rules and dictating what your kids can spend their money on is all it takes to teach your children financial responsibility, but it isn't. Just like you and me, kids learn infinitely more through personal experience than they do from having someone tell them what to do.

Therefore, your job as the CEO is to run The Family Bank by the same "big boy and big girl" rules by which you live. As your kids get themselves into varying degrees of financial difficulty, then, and only then, will you be able to take notes, develop lesson plans, organize your Weekly Meetings and teach those lessons about responsibility that you are dying to teach. But remember, try to distinguish between teaching your children how to be responsible and teaching your children about economic theory.

I encourage you to encourage your kids to venture out and explore all levels of fiscal responsibility. Let them get into massive debt, and then teach them how to work their way out of it. Let them be stingy and burn some bridges (by not buying presents or whatever), and then teach them that they have to honor social obligations. In the end, your children will settle into the comfortable and relatively stress-free life that can only be achieved through a balanced budget. Once your children figure out for themselves (probably around age fifteen to sixteen) how to live a balanced and responsible financial life, then that lifestyle won't change just because they turn eighteen years old and get real credit. Allow yourself to allow your children to make the mistakes that we all have to make, but allow them do it under the protection of The Family Bank. Remember, all the mistakes they make at home are learning experiences that will cause no lasting damage financially, but the lessons they will learn are invaluable.

Let's bottom line this "Mentor" thing. The Family Bank is meant to teach your kids how to make money and how to spend it; so save the lessons on economic philosophy for a little later. Let them use The Family Bank and abuse it, but most of all let them learn from it. Mentor them and guide them, but don't control them.

Chapter 4

The Parent: Retaining your Identity

The Family Bank is an investment. You are giving up (investing) your power as a parent to veto your child's purchases, for a much more valuable "return", which is your child's ability to control his money and to utilize the modern financial system to his benefit.

It's important to understand how to be a parent during both the roles of CEO and of the Mentor. Let's pretend for a minute that you (The Family Bank aside) have just purchased a brand new, big screen television, or let's say, a pair of $500 shoes. When you make a large purchase you feel a little . . . let's call it "euphoric" on the drive home. You are happy to finally have that big item that you've been wanting, and if someone tries to tell you (during the ride home) that you could have saved 10% somewhere else, or that that purchase might not have been wise at that moment, you probably won't be keen on hearing it right then. So where is this going? When your son uses The Family Bank to purchase an item at the toy store that you believe is a waste of money, you will act as the CEO and facilitate the transaction. You won't give on-the-spot mentoring advice. Simply take quick notes and save the mentoring for your upcoming Weekly Meeting.

Your role as Mentor will only be during the Weekly Meetings, because if you allow some time to pass between the acts of purchasing a frivolous item and "mentoring" your son about the purchase, he is much more likely to heed your mentoring advice. This brings us back to my example of purchasing that large dollar item you've been eyeing for some time. A couple of days after the purchase, when the novelty has worn off, you might listen to your spouse's "more rational" advice and kick yourself for not waiting until the item went on sale, or for not shopping around a little more. We always think more rationally about a big purchase a couple days after the fact, and it's the same for your kids. This is why you want to wait to talk to them until the Weekly Meeting.

Banks don't regulate your purchases on the spot, so you **cannot** regulate your son's purchases either! This will be painful to watch for you at first, as he blows literally tens of dollars on junk; but keep in mind that just because you can't stop him from buying candy, does *NOT* mean you can't stop him from eating it! You're only the CEO during financial transactions; at all other times you're still his parent. In fact, the first time my daughter bought candy I purchased it, issued her a receipt for it, and when we walked out of the store I told her that I didn't give her permission to buy the candy and I threw it in the trash! She cried, but she also learned that just because she has total control over her money doesn't mean that she has no rules! *More importantly, though*, she also learned that The Family Bank is **not** going to stop her from making bad decisions and "throwing away" her money!

One important point here is that you can never mix the rolls of banker and parent at the same time. You *CANNOT* say "I'll give you the money if you really want it, but as your Dad I'm telling you that you're not allowed to buy this." The purpose of The Family Bank is for her to make the mistakes early and learn from them early. Throwing away $20 dollars today is better than throwing away $20k twelve years from now. However, if your daughter asks you if she can buy something before she actually buys it, then you will say, "You can spend your money however you want." The only time you will confiscate an item she purchases or tell her, "No, you are not allowed to buy that", is when she wants to purchase a "contraband" item. Contraband items are only those items that she is not allowed to own because they are illegal, unhealthful, or items you object to morally or religiously. For example, you can ban inappropriate clothing, but you cannot ban excessive spending on appropriate clothing. I hope this section on banning *only* contraband and nothing else makes sense to you and that you embrace it, because if you are still clinging to the idea that you want to regulate every purchase, then I have failed in explaining to you the importance of letting your children learn from their own mistakes early in life and under your protection.

The Bottom Line: During the Weekly Meeting you are the Mentor and at all other times you are the CEO of the Family Bank. However, you are always her parent, too. If she is trying to buy something that you have forbidden her to buy (contraband), like candy or a mini skirt, then you will allow her to buy it, because you are the CEO and she is using the Family Bank properly. However, immediately after the purchase you will confiscate the item as her Parent, and you can even return it and keep the money (she spent the money, so it's gone). The Family Bank will never trump your role as her Parent. Actually, you have created your Family Bank because you are a responsible parent, so naturally, the roles of CEO and Mentor are just tools to help you be the best parent possible. As the CEO you will allow her to utilize The Family Bank at all times, however she wants; as the Mentor you will teach her how the world works during your Weekly Meetings, and as her Parent you set and enforce the rules at all times. Remember, just because you (as the CEO) allow your daughter to make financial mistakes and spend her money on contraband, it does not mean that you (as her Parent) will allow her to have contraband items.

Chapter 5

Setting up The Family Bank

Your Business Front—The Body

This is the easy part. To get started you need to build the "(your name here) Family Bank", and here we're talking about designating a physical location. All businesses have a location; even Internet businesses run from a home, and have an area of the home designated for business. Whether you're fortunate enough to have your own office in your house, or even if you have to designate a corner of your kitchen in your one-bedroom apartment, the location is irrelevant. What's important is that you have a designated location that your kids can grow up identifying as The (your last name here) Family Bank. Create a sign or nameplate for your Family Bank, and voila, you're the proud owner of your very own (your name here) Family Bank.

Setting up the framework of your Family Bank is very simple. The Family Bank is completely your own, so run wild with it and turn it into whatever works for you. At a minimum, you will need a few items: journals, a dry erase board, notebooks, an "in and out" box, a lock-box, a cork board and some scrap paper.

Ideally, you will have a desk centered in the middle of an office facing the door, not against any walls, with a little sign or nameplate on it that says (your name) Family Bank. You'll also have an inbox and outbox tray on the desk, a locking drawer in the desk designated as your vault, and your white board hanging on the wall behind your desk with your cork board next to it. This setup facilitates a formal feeling anytime your kids come in to deal with The Family Bank. If Miss Thrifty wants to apply for a loan, then she can pull a small uncomfortable chair up to your desk and fill out the paperwork right in front of you. Then you can look it over to make sure it's filled out correctly and set the application in your inbox with a polite, "We'll get back to you when we've processed your application." The setup of your Family Bank is completely up to you, but keep in mind that the more formal you create the feel of your bank, the better prepared your child will be the first time she walks into a job interview or into a bank to apply for that first used car loan.

The White Board—The Face]

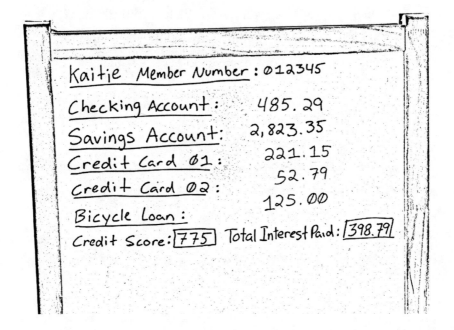

This is where you'll display your account member's checking account balance, savings account balance, credit card balance, loan balances, and credit score, for him, and the world, to see. It's basically like your online Family Bank home page, but for your kids. By having all their numbers up on the whiteboard for them to see every day, it will serve as a constant reminder that they can never escape financial responsibility and that even though their money is not in their hands, it is, in fact, still real. If you begin The Family Bank at the ideal time, when your child is eight years old, then he will already be struggling with the idea of giving up physical control of his money; thus, the whiteboard becomes his link to his money. The whiteboard is truly the face of your Family Bank. Without the whiteboard the entire Family Bank system remains an amorphous concept that children will not be able to visualize or truly understand.

The Journal—The Heart

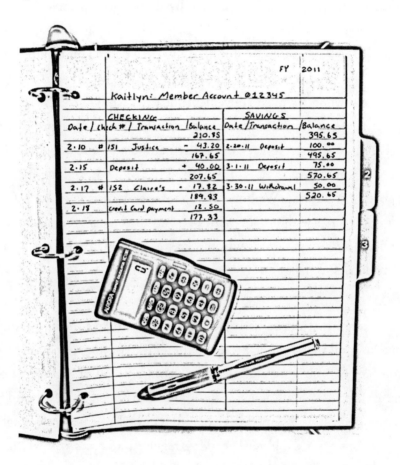

We've discussed the journal a little bit already, but this is the heart of the Family Bank and Financial System. Your knowledge and experience is the soul of The Family Bank, but your ability to maintain order and to convey that wisdom to your children is what gives life to this system. The very day you allow yourself to get disorganized and confused is the day your kids will lose faith in The Family Bank. When Miss Thrifty comes to check on her account and apply for a loan, but you have to ask her to see her notebook because you don't know how much money she has in her checking account, well, you'll see a look of confusion and disappointment you don't want to see. Business owners, especially bank owners, live and die by their organizational skills. If you're not a particularly organized individual, then pay close attention to how to lay out your journal and DON'T fall behind on making your entries. If your kids needed medication to survive, would you only give it to them when it's most convenient for you? No, your kids are your priority, so you have to make their financial future your priority, as well. You don't want to get disorganized and come across looking like a fool to your fifteen-year-old, whom we all know is looking for that opportunity, anyway. We know that banks truly survive on faith (and accounting), so without the faith of your customers, your bank will die. Keep a journal, keep it tidy and keep it up to date; you won't have many entries to make, so stay on top of it.

If keeping a journal is beginning to sound like too much work, keep in mind that your eight-year-old might make one purchase every month or two, so we're talking about a commitment of approximately one minute per month, here. Becoming proficient as CEO of The Family Bank is not something you are required to master overnight. By the time your daughter is making regular purchases you will have been running The Family Bank for probably about six years! I promise you that when you open your Family Bank you will be able to quickly and easily manage the details of running The Family Bank to include maintaining your journal.

The Family Bank

You will use your journal to record every single transaction your bank members make. You will need to separate your journal into multiple sections:

1. Daily Transactions (checking and savings)

2. Daily Transactions (credit cards and loans)

3. Notes

You will keep records for:

- Savings

- Checking

- Credit Cards

- Loans

I personally have to use one three ring binder with three tabs as my journal, in order to keep all her transactions orderly. One is for her checking and savings, one for her credit and loans and one for notes. This works for me, but how you organize your journal or journals is completely up to you.

Not all transactions will be "initiated" by your son, either, so you will have to pay special attention to interest charges when recording all transactions. All credit transactions have to be separate from checking account transactions, so you can calculate interest charges, just like your bank does. You don't want to confuse what your kids are purchasing with their own money, versus what they are buying on credit. This is why I use a separate section in my notebook for credit transactions. Also, keep in mind that you won't even begin using credit in The Family Bank until you've been running your bank for years, so don't feel overwhelmed.

The notes section is where you'll record your observations, such as "Miss Thrifty is considering not buying birthday presents this year to save money. I need to talk to her about considering a small loan she can handle and how it's better to give than to receive, etc . . ." or "Mr. Reckless does not understand that he is maxing out his credit . . ." By the way, Mr. Reckless is **not** a nickname; **never** nickname your kids in your journal! Nicknames are judgmental and inevitably your children will look through it someday when you're not home. Label them as Mr. or Miss (their last name), keeping everything absolutely professional. Your bank members need to feel some "butterflies" when they have to go into an interview with you and the only way to do that is to make every single interaction with The Family Bank absolutely realistic and, above all, professional. Basically, keep your notes orderly, current and professional.

Above all else, find a method to the madness of keeping your journal. This process will be trial and error at first and luckily it starts out very slowly. My three ring binder is large and cumbersome, and not very practical to take with me to the store when I go shopping with my daughter, so another great tool to help keep you organized is a small, portable day planner for when you leave the house. I use a day planner with a calendar and a notes section at the end. This way, when I record an "on the spot" transaction in a store, I just write it on that calendar day along with my notes in the notes section. Remember to jot down your thoughts about your child's purchases, so you don't forget to discuss it at your upcoming Weekly Meeting. For example, I took notes when my daughter spent every penny in her account on candy! This only takes 30 seconds (both my notes and my eight-year-old spending all her money!) Then, at the end of the week I look over The Family Bank day planner, transcribe my notes into my permanent journal and create my lesson plan for our 8am Saturday morning Weekly Meeting. When it comes to the particulars about your journal, how you organize it is up to you, but remember:

- It must be accurate and up to date at all times

- You must notate all the details of every transaction to include date, time, location and method of payment

- You must take quick notes on the spending habits of your children

- Everything that ends up on the whiteboard must also have a permanent record in your journal, and vice-versa

Don't forget, the whiteboard will look like an online bank statement, but the way you keep your permanent records must be more like your monthly bank statements. All the credit card charges, debit charges, checks, ATM withdrawals and, later on, loan information, must all be separated out into their own columns or even in their own journals. Remember that when you start The Family Bank your daughter will only be making approximately one transaction every month or two, and credit won't be introduced until years down the road. In the beginning you will only be recording and entering one transaction every couple of months, so you'll have years of practice keeping your journal before your records get more complicated. By then you will be an expert and you'll be able to maintain your journal in your sleep.

You may decide to maintain your journals on your home computer and record all transactions onto easy-to-read spreadsheets, which is a great idea! But remember to backup all your information onto an external drive every day. We need to be an example of stability for our customers; after all, banks don't forgive loans just because their computers crash!

The Notebook (not your journal)—The Backbone

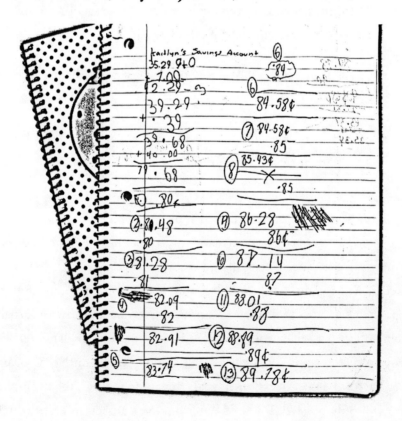

Do you remember the olden days of the "check register"? Yup, that little book you used to write down the dollar amount of every check you wrote, along with the date, the check number and to whom you wrote the check. And who can forget the fun that came from that magical moment of trying to "balance" it! Well, the notebook is the same special little treat, but for your bank customer to record all of her transactions. Her notebook is where all the abstract financial transactions become real and where everything she has learned and all her experiences get cemented into her brain. Without your child keeping a visual, permanent record of every transaction, every purchase and every withdrawal, she will never be able to see the long-term big picture of how her spending habits affect her personal wealth. And yes, when you sit down with your kids and talk about their money, refer to it as their personal wealth. The word wealth is more meaningful than the word money, and it's like a little pat on the back for a job well done saving their money.

Reviewing his notebook should happen at the beginning of each Weekly Meeting. This acts as a great lead-in to your Mentoring session. Take this time to verify that the records are correct and up to date, fix anything or add anything that needs it, and then ask your son how he feels his financial situation is coming along. At first you'll hear a lot of "I don't know", which is fine, but as you progress into the system and your kids get a little older you'll start to get the questions you've been waiting for, like, "Why don't I ever have enough money?" and, "What do I need to do to save enough money to start my own business?" Okay, that last one's a ways off, but hearing these questions is both your goal and your opportunity, because they signify that your child is ready for some discussion on long-term financial planning. Use his notebook as a tangible tool to teach him the organizational skills he will need, and to give him a concrete reminder that financial responsibility is a daily requirement.

Your child's notebook is used to teach both the obvious lesson of organization and the more subtle lesson of learning how to budget. Here is an example of using her notebook to teach her a tangible lesson on budgeting during a Weekly Meeting. If you have ever gone into a car dealership to buy a car, then I'm sure you've encountered a salesman who first asked you what your "price range" was, and then immediately showed you a car that was above that range. Of course you loved the car, but then you began that internal debate about whether or not you could really afford it. That internal debate stems from wanting something, plus having only a general idea of your own financial situation (not having a solid budget). Not sure about that last statement? Have you ever stopped to do the math in order to determine if you could afford a 50 million dollar home? No? That's because you already know with certainty that you cannot afford it, which is exactly what we're talking about here. With a solid budget your daughter will know with certainty that her limit is $300 per month and not $305 per month.

Okay, now back to the car salesman who chimes in with, "The payment might look like a lot, but all you have to do to make the payment on that beautiful new car is to cut out that daily cup of coffee you grab on the way to work." Then, magically, you'll have all the extra money you need to make that car payment, right? Did that really help you? It probably didn't, because it was an intangible and unrealistic statement; but it did serve its purpose of fueling your internal debate. How much do you really spend on coffee? Could it really add up to $100 per month? And could you realistically cut it out? A solid budget is the only way to answer that question.

When your daughter walks into a car dealership, someday, you don't want her to have any doubt or question about exactly how much money she can comfortably afford to pay for a car. Teaching her how to use her notebook effectively is how you will teach her to know her limits. Use what you've learned from experience and point out in your child's notebook the purchases she's made that didn't benefit her in the long run. Then talk to her about whether or not those purchases are truly necessary. Some kids spend too much money going out to lunch and on their hobbies, others spend too much on clothes and video games. The concept you want to hold in the back of your mind while you are reviewing your child's notebook with her during the Weekly Meeting, is your desire to impress upon her how much money she is actually spending every week and what those expenses are doing to her personal wealth.

Her notebook will be her first version of a budget that she encounters and you want her to begin to see it that way. She writes all her financial transactions in her notebook, to include her paycheck deposits, so it's a short leap from there to actually writing out and summing up all her bills. That way she'll have a projection of her available spending money every month.

Have your daughter analyze her notebook during your Weekly Meetings, and have her think about her financial priorities. Once she comes to the realization that her income is limited she will be faced with some age old dilemmas: whether she is happier buying new toys or wearing nicer clothes, wearing nicer clothes or driving a nicer car, driving a nicer car or going to a better college. Make her think about how much money she makes and where her money is actually going. As you review her notebook every week, you can point to the black-and-white, and show her where her spending needs to be reduced in order to reach her financial goals. All this will seem pointless with your eight-year-old, but get her used to the process early. By the time she is fifteen years old, this notebook and budget analysis will be second nature to her, which will be a major win for you!

A word of caution: this notebook will start out as a huge mess and it's up to you to teach her how to organize it. When she loses track of her money, take the time to get her re-organized. When she comes to you for the 30th Weekly Meeting in a row and her notebook is still a mess, be patient; she'll get to where she needs to be, eventually. Once your daughter gets the knack of successfully keeping all her records straight and she's been keeping her notebook well organized for about a year, then it's time to make her officially accountable for her notebook. Explain to her, during a Weekly Meeting, that she has been doing a great job of keeping her records in her notebook, and from now on she is solely in charge of keeping her records in order. If she ends up messing up her records after that, then she'll have to call you and set up a special mid-week appointment to come in and see the CEO. She will have to dress up and show up on time to her appointment, and then you'll walk her through all her transactions and get her notebook back in order. I remember having to do this once or twice with my bank, and just like then, once she is all straightened out you will charge her a small consultation fee of $5 and deduct it straight out of her checking account (off the whiteboard). She'll learn accountability quickly, because no one likes paying fees!

Scrap Paper, Pens, Tape, Scissors—The Central Nervous System

Office supplies and a computer (if you've got one) are what make The Family Bank move, act and react. You will use simple everyday supplies to create a checkbook, debit card, credit card, draft loan papers, make receipts, and do everything else that you can dream up to make The Family Bank function to its maximum potential. If you are thinking that you *have* to be able to get your child online, show them online banking, get them real "plastic" issued from your bank and print official loan applications in order to be successful with The Family Bank, then you are dead wrong, (although you definitely *can* do all that). You are teaching your children basic principles about money management, basic investing and how to avoid getting in debt over their heads. Kids have imaginations that adults literally cannot imagine. Also, if you are under the impression that your kids will have a leg up if they have the use of tons of technology, you are, again, sadly mistaken. In fact, if you do utilize technology, be very careful not to rely too heavily on your kids "going online and learning on their own." From my experience, the children that learn the best are the ones who get the most face time with their parents. So consider this, even if money is no object and your kids have all the technology in the world; when you first open The Family Bank, sit down with your kids and some scrap paper and make everything you need for your bank by hand. Obviously, you don't have to do this, especially if you are starting up your bank and your son is already sixteen years old, but consider it. A little time together can't hurt. Besides, once you have made everything by hand, later on down the road you can replace homemade supplies with more official looking materials, but it is not at all necessary to do so.

Due to the fact that technology and computers are so prevalent today, I am going to cover two ways of creating The Family Bank materials: the low tech way and the high tech way.

Low Tech: To start up your bank you will need to create a checking and a savings account; therefore, a check book and a debit card. I'm not going to waste your time here telling you how to make those, just pull them out of your wallet and draw what you see on the scrap paper (with your kid's information in there), then cut them out and laminate them, using clear tape if you have to. Now you're ready to get started.

High Tech: To start you will need all the same supplies as you did for the low tech. However, go to your bank (either online or in person) and get copies of their loan applications for their checking and savings account. Using the real forms as a template and create your own bank letterhead on your computer and fill in the "guts" of the applications onto your Family Bank paperwork.

Next, go online and open for your kids their own checking and savings accounts in their own names and order checks and debit cards for them. Once you've opened real checking accounts for them, you can go online to check printing companies and order customized checks for your kids in their names, with their account numbers.

An important word of caution here: you are solely and completely in charge of and responsible for the real accounts you create for your children. Your children are not allowed to make any purchases or use their real accounts in any way while you are running The Family Bank. The purpose of the real checks is to acquaint your children with what the real financial tools look like and how they work, not to really use them in real stores. I will explain how you will have your children use the real tools in the Checking Account chapter, but if you get them real debit cards and real checks, then there is always the possibility that they will try to *really* use them at a store. Make it crystal clear to your children that using them for real is not authorized, and always monitor their accounts for unauthorized spending. The reason you need to keep complete control is because they are banking through you, The Family Bank, not your real bank. Any mistakes they make through The Family Bank are controlled and overseen by you. I really like the idea of going with all real materials, but again, your kids are using The Family Bank, not your real bank.

Many banks allow you to open separate accounts for your children, and I highly encourage you to do this. However, because every bank is different, I can't go into too much depth regarding what you can or should do online, but take advantage of all the tools you have at your disposal. If your bank allows you to get a prepaid credit card for your kids, then absolutely take advantage of this. You can prepay the card from your personal account, but don't make your kids prepay the card because that defeats the purpose of a "credit card". With a Family Bank credit card you are extending a line of credit to your kids via The Family Bank and using a real credit card adds a tremendous sense of realism. If you make your daughter prepay her card, though, then she knows it's not credit because she already paid for it. Ideally, through your bank you will be able to obtain a debit card for your child's checking account, and a prepaid credit card and real checks, so she will have a realistic sense of the tools adults use to control their money.

If you like the idea of realistic checks, but don't want "real" checks, you can either create your own Family Bank checks on your computer, or download some realistic checks from the Internet. Many websites have free downloadable "kid checks" that look pretty realistic, but no one will confuse them with real bank checks. Your own imagination and creativity are your only limits here.

We touched on this earlier, but I want to differentiate between using technology to your advantage and relying on technology to do all the work of The Family Bank for you. Keeping a paper journal of all your records will work perfectly on its own, but ideally, your Family Bank and Financial System will be able to incorporate both the use of technology and your home computer. Hopefully, you have a computer available where you can generate items like bank forms and loan applications. If you're computer savvy, you can tackle bigger projects like walking your kids through creating a business proposal presentation for starting their own businesses, although that won't be until the later years when you get them to the more advanced stages of The Family Financial System.

Technology can be incredibly useful, as long as you don't replace yourself with it. Avoid finding financial programs that teach your kids lessons online, and just having your kids run through them. The Family Bank is about passing your unique wisdom on to your kids, not just increasing their homework load. As I'm sure you can see, your imagination and dedication are literally the only limits to The Family Bank and Financial System, and to what your children can learn and accomplish by using it.

Online Banking (Whiteboard)—

Online banking is where all our banking transactions are headed in the near future. Your children's ability to remotely access and manipulate their bank accounts is important. We can't exactly give a laptop to an eight-year-old, so we have to teach them the principles of online banking without a computer. Until your kids are old enough to own and use their own computer (and even after that), being able to see their balances, recent transactions, and general interactions with The Family Bank, displayed on the whiteboard, is essential. It's important to acquaint your children early on with the idea of their personal information being readily available online. Remember, all the sections in your journal, except your notes, have to be represented on the whiteboard.

Each morning after having issued a receipt the day before, whether it is for a purchase, deposit or whatever, you have to remember to update the whiteboard. Your bank updates your online accounts every day; therefore, so do you. How do you remember to do this every day? Look in your journal every morning before you head to work and make it a part of your morning routine. In your journal you will have written every transaction made the day before, and, of course, the dates of every transaction will be labeled (which is why I like to use a day planner with a calendar) in case you miss a day or two. The whiteboard is your child's connection to his money. It's his online bank, so remember to keep it current.

For their checking accounts, the whiteboard always displays the current standing of their accounts, to include their balances and a couple recent transactions: deposits, ATM withdrawals, overdraft fees, checks and debit card purchases. You only have to maintain a couple of transactions on the board, because all the transactions should be recorded in both their notebooks and your journal.

For their savings accounts, the whiteboard should show their balances and the last couple deposits and withdrawals. For loans and credit cards it should show the balances and the last couple transactions: charges, payments or interest charges. Remember, you should update the board every morning, just like your bank does with your accounts. This isn't as time consuming as it sounds, as your elementary school child won't be writing more than one check every month or so, but it will pick up as they get older.

Warning: remember that kids are kids and one day they are inevitably going to try to "alter" the numbers while you're not home. This will be a rough day. First, you keep accurate records, so you will always be able to notice and correct the error the next morning, when you notice the whiteboard doesn't match your journal. Second, financial crimes are outside the jurisdiction of The Family Bank, because they are a criminal offense. This is where the "Family Sheriff" has to step in and take over. Basically, the little cyber-criminal just has to be punished. The Family Bank is not about punishment, but keep in mind that in this case it should mimic real life consequences and should be proportional to the amount "stolen". The fact that altering numbers is a crime should be discussed at some point in a Weekly Meeting, so there are no surprises when their real life punishment and restitution overlap with The Family Bank.

An Inbox / Outbox—Ummm . . . what part of the body is the Outbox? . . .

Let's see . . . it's where all the paperwork goes after your customer feeds the system by writing you a check, submitting a loan application, etc. It's just a tray with your customer's name on it that sits on your Family Bank desk, or wherever your Family Bank is located. For example, after your daughter writes you a check and you "process" the check overnight (deduct the amount from her account), you put the cashed check into the Outbox for your daughter to pick up later for her records.

Besides the Outbox, you will also maintain an Inbox. As you might imagine, the Inbox is where your daughter can leave a filled-out account application, employment application, or anything else she wants processed by The Family Bank.

SECTION II

Moving and Controlling Money

The ideal age for a new customer to open her first account is around seven or eight years old. This lets both of you ease into the concept of The Family Bank and Financial System at right about the age when your daughter has learned and become somewhat proficient with addition and subtraction in school.

At the core of The Family Bank and Financial System is the concept of controlling money via a third party, The Family Bank. Remember how much you hated the idea of letting your parents "hold on" to that $20 you got on your birthday, because you weren't really sure if you'd ever see it again? And if your Mom bought you those $80 shoes you had been asking for, was that $20 in her pocket still yours? The key to success here is always trying to remember how you used to see the world at eight years old, and then tailor your mentoring sessions to help your kids better understand why the financial system works the way it does. The bottom line is that kids think and rationalize everything in a linear manner. For example, "I have $20, so I need to be holding on to my $20 or it won't be mine anymore." This leads us into the first functional step of The Family Bank: the savings account.

Explaining the function of a bank and a savings account, at eight years old, nonetheless, is hands down the most difficult Mentoring session you will have. As we discussed earlier, you will have Weekly Meetings, or Mentoring sessions, with each account holder individually, before you can implement each new instrument in The Family Bank. Before you hand your eight-year-old little girl her first Family Bank notebook, you have to thoroughly explain what it is and how it works. Try not to focus on the philosophy behind banking in your first Weekly Meeting. It's too complicated, and they really won't care, anyway.

Your first mentoring session will be when you feel your child is starting to understand the concept of numbers and counting, and when he demonstrates that he understands that numbers are a representation of something real, physical and tangible. I found that the first time your son asks you to buy something for him because it "only costs $5" is the prime time to start!

The first mentoring session should now be as soon as possible, the first time you can spare 30 minutes to an hour, like a Saturday morning or whatever time works for your family. Tell your son or daughter that you're going to teach him/her about how money works and how to become a member of the (Last name) Family Bank. Sometime that week, go and set up the physical location of your Family Bank, unless, of course, you have already been running the Family Bank for an older child. When it comes time for your first Weekly Meeting, you will need to explain five topics to her:

1. The location of The Family Bank.

2. From here on out, this is where her money will be kept.

3. The Family Bank will keep her money safe. This is when you show her a little safe or a locking drawer in your desk and tell her that this is the safe where her money will be stored. Kids need to see something tangible and seemingly independent from your "pockets", as far as where their $20 dollars is going to end up. Explain that when she carries around cash or leaves it in her room, sometimes she'll lose it or other people will find it and take it. In order to keep their money safe, everyone puts their money in a bank. Banks promise that the money people give them will always be safe and available when needed. Even

if someone breaks into the bank and steals the bank's money, the bank will always make sure that she gets her money back.

4. The Family Bank will count her money and maintain accurate records of her money every day. Explain that as she makes more and more money, it will become very difficult to keep track of exactly how much money she has, and that she won't have the time to sit and count all her cash before each time she goes shopping. Banks keep her money counted for her all the time, and all she'll have to do is look at her bank account to see how much money she has.

5. Finally, explain that banks pay her money, to hold on to her money. Don't go into detail about interest or how banks make money by reinvesting the money she gives them; that will be a topic for a much later date.

Once you've fielded all the questions about why The Family Bank is taking away all her money, it's time to explain how she will have access to her money whenever she needs it. Let's start with her savings account. You may feel you need to break up the above conversation and the following discussion regarding banking and her savings account into two Weekly Meetings and that is perfectly fine, especially if you are starting your child in The Family Bank at seven or eight years old. If your child is already ten years old when you read this book, then let's throw all this together and keep moving along.

Chapter 6

Savings Account

During the first or second "orientation" Weekly Meeting you will explain that in order to use The Family Bank, and impress upon her that she *wants* to use The Family Bank, she must fill out an application for a Family Bank Savings Account. Explain that a savings account is a way to access the money she is holding at the bank. When she opens a savings account, the bank assigns her and her money a number called a savings account number. From that point on, every time she goes to the bank or calls her bank on the phone, she just has to give them her "account number" and they will have all her information and the information about her money readily available. Another function of the savings account is that every month she lets her money sit in her savings account the bank will pay her a little bit of money for letting the money stay there. This is called interest.

I recommend using a (follow me here) 1% *monthly* rate, compounded weekly, for your child's savings account interest rate. This may seem astronomically high, but you are using a basic reward versus punishment model to teach your children the benefits of positive interest from saving money, versus negative interest from borrowing money. Your children need to see a substantial reward for saving money and they need to see it in relatively short increments of time. The reason you need to compound the interest weekly is that children have a very short attention span and need to be able to "see" the positive interest accumulate each and every week. Think back to elementary school; do you remember how long each school year seemed? Like an eternity. But now that we are older, the years just seem to fly by. Well, we need to tailor The Family Bank to feel proportional to that "younger" perspective of time. So, by compounding her interest weekly, instead of monthly like real banks, you give your kids a reward that they have to wait for, but not wait so long that they forget what they were waiting for to begin with.

A 1% monthly interest rate compounded weekly might seem really high, but remember that one of the main points of The Family Bank is to make your kids want to save money and to keep saving, and the dollar amounts we are talking about here won't "break your bank." If your son has a hundred dollars in savings, then at the end of the week you will calculate a quarter of one percent [1 percent of 100 = 1 dollar, and 1 dollar divided by 4 weeks = 25 cents], and add that to his account. The formula you will use is:

- **His account balance multiplied by 1.0025 (every week)**

So, at the end of that week you will throw a quarter into the safe (remember to keep the money in the safe equal to or greater than the numbers on the white board) and then add the 25 cents to her account on the whiteboard (in black marker) and label it as "interest payment". Remember to tell your daughter that every week she leaves her money in The Family Bank she will receive an interest payment for her money and the more money she has in the bank, the bigger the payment will become.

Last, but not least, it's important to set the record straight from the very beginning that a bank is a professional organization, like any business. Explain that people work there and people have to be respectful and dress nicely when they go to a bank. Also, when you deal with the bank you call the people working there Sir or Ma'am, or you call them by their title (Mr. or Ms.) and their last name. Then practice this. Go sit at the desk and tell your daughter to come in and ask for Mr. (your last name), and to tell you that she would like to submit an application for a savings account. Now that she knows what a savings account is, you will present her with one of your homemade / computer generated savings account applications. Sit with her and help her fill it out by asking her the questions on the form and filling in the answers with her, then let her sign her name on the bottom of the application.

After she stumbles through that, thank her for the application, tell her she has been approved, and take her $20 dollars or however much she has to open her account. Put the money directly into your Family Bank "safe" and write her brand new account number on the whiteboard (in blue) and the amount of the money in her account (in black) next to her account number (her balance).

Inform her that if she wants to take money out of her account all she has to do is schedule an appointment with you for a time she can come into The Family Bank and withdraw some of her money.

Explain to her that after every withdrawal she makes, you will log it in your journal and notate it on the whiteboard (in red), next to her new balance (in black).

At this point, you will give your daughter her notebook and explain that she also has to write every transaction down in her notebook, and then show her how to do it. Don't worry about making her understand exactly how to keep her journal orderly and current, because you will be spending the next few years trying to teach her that lesson.

You may or may not have noticed that after all my reminders not to mix the roles of the Mentor and the CEO, I went ahead and mixed the roles of the Mentor and the CEO in one of the first Weekly Meetings (when you help your son fill out his first application for a savings account with The Family Bank). That wasn't a mistake. You won't draw that hard line in the sand between Mentor and CEO until you are sure that your son has a firm grasp of how to use and maintain his savings account. This Weekly Meeting, when your son fills out his savings account application, is when you will teach your son that you in fact have two roles within The Family Bank. You'll teach him that you are just his Mom or Dad (Mentor) during these Weekly Meetings, but that when he interacts with The Family Bank at any other time he has to call you Mr. or Ms. (your last name), because at those times you are his banker.

During this orientation to the Family Bank process it is important to give your son something tangible (the savings account application and his notebook), while at the same time explaining in a friendly, fatherly tone "what it all means" and how to use it. You will play the role of CEO while your son fills out his savings account application during this Weekly Meeting so you can show him how The Family Bank will continue to work from that point. This will be the only time that mixing of the Mentor and CEO roles happens. It is important to give him the following: the orientation, the tangible items like his notebook and savings account application, and an example of how it all works, all at the same time, in order to tie it all together for him.

A word of WARNING here: This whole orientation process will **not** go smoothly with a seven—or eight-year-old, but that's okay! Fumble through it once and then in Weekly Meeting number two or three, depending on how you broke them up, go over the entire orientation again and re-explain every aspect of the savings account . . . again. Show him how to fill out the application again and how to write the transactions in his notebook, again. Continue to run him through the orientation until it makes sense to him, but don't go over the entire orientation more than once in one Weekly Meeting or you will see tears!

The concept of The Family Bank is complicated to a seven—or eight-year-old at its inception, but that does not mean you should wait until he's older to do it. By introducing your children to The Family Bank early on, it will seem to them that financial responsibility is all they have ever known, and *that* alone is worth its weight in gold. The moral here is to be patient and remember that The Family Bank is a lot for an eight-year-old to grasp, but once you see your son finally maintaining his notebook by himself, it will be well worth it!

Also, remember that no matter what happens in The Family Bank, neither you nor your children should ever feel rushed or stressed. The Family Bank is a long-term project and if any Weekly Meeting is not going how you want it to go, because either you feel your lesson is not clear or your child is getting frustrated and not understanding what you are teaching, you can always cut the Weekly Meeting short and start over again next week. We don't want any hard feelings on either side. You have plenty of time to achieve your goals; even if your child is fifteen years old when you open your branch of The Family Bank, you have plenty of time.

Now your bank is open for business, your child is up to speed on the basics of a savings account and you have successfully completed your first few Weekly Meetings. Congratulations, the hardest part is over!

Let's recap what we've covered so far in your Weekly Meeting orientation week. First, you showed her where The Family Bank is located and explained what The Family Bank is, why she should use it and that the bank actually pays her to leave her money in a savings account. Second, you helped her get started by showing her how to open her first savings account and you showed her how to keep her own records of her accounts. Third, you explained that a bank is a business and when she goes to the bank she is dealing with business professionals, so she has to dress nicely and act politely and professionally. Finally, you taught her that you are the CEO of The Family Bank and that when she deals with you as the CEO she must not think of you as Mom or Dad. When she goes to the bank, she will think of you as (and call you) Mr. or Ms. (your last name).

Chapter 7

Checking Account

Eventually, maybe sooner rather than later depending on what age you start your child in The Family Bank, you are going to either see frustration from your son when he wants to buy something, but doesn't have cash with him, or in a Weekly Meeting he will just bring up the inconvenience of having to go to The Family Bank to withdraw the money. Enter . . . The Family Bank Checking Account. Use the next Weekly Meeting as an opportunity to explain what a "checking account" is and how to use it.

During this checking account meeting, unlike with the initial savings account meeting, you will tell your son that he needs to schedule an appointment with the CEO of The Family Bank, and get cleaned up and dressed up in order to go into The Family Bank to apply for a checking account. Schedule this time for whenever it is convenient for you and let it play out. When he comes into The Family Bank and asks for a checking account application, treat it just like a real life situation. Help him fill out the application and have him sign it (remember you are filing every application your kids give you in a permanent file, never throwing away a single sheet of paper your kids turn in to you). Then you approve your son's new checking account and give your son his first, either homemade or bank generated, "(Your Last Name) Family Bank" checkbook and debit card (with PIN).

You should make the checkbook and debit card as accurate as possible, as we discussed earlier, but don't photocopy any real documents here; this isn't a lesson in how the Secret Service works! Just make sure that your checks have a check number (top and bottom), "to" line, date, amount both written and numeric, a "memo" line (that unnecessary line at the bottom left, which is actually a really good idea for your kids to fill in), a routing number (your Family Bank number) and the account number at the bottom of the check. During your next Weekly Meeting take the time to explain all these parts of a check to your son and let him practice filling it in until he gets the hang of it. He doesn't have to be a perfectly proficient check writer, because you'll be there to help him every time he writes one.

The checkbook and debit card work like this: whenever Mr. Reckless or Miss Thrifty want to buy something at the store with you, they either have to write you a check or swipe their debit card with you (they can just show you their debit card and tell you they are using it to buy the item). In turn, you issue them a receipt for the item; you can give them the real receipt if you like. After your child makes the purchase of an item with The Family Bank, you then have to purchase that item. Remember, you will be keeping all the real money your bank members give you locked up in The Family Bank vault at home. It's imperative that anytime your child wants to buy something, regardless of how frivolous or wasteful, you always have the money with you to make the purchase on the spot. Again, this should not be a problem, because you will always have your child's money locked up safely at home. If money is tight for you, then keep Mr. Reckless' Family Bank account money with you when you leave the house.

Also, explain that when his money is sitting in a checking account it doesn't accrue interest the way it does in a savings account. The benefit, of course, is that the bank gives him tools to be able to use his money any time he wants to, so it is a trade-off of benefits for efficiency. There are two points here: first, I know your checking account might give you some interest, but again, you are teaching simple lessons here, so keeping the interest on his checking account at zero will more clearly illustrate the purpose and function of a checking account, which is to have readily available access to the funds in his account. Second, if your kids are old enough, you can take this opportunity to explain that because money in a savings account is not intended to be used on a daily basis (hence the term "savings" account) the bank has more opportunity to invest this money in order to make money for themselves, and in turn pay your son for this opportunity to use his money. On the other hand, if his money is in a checking account it means the money will be spent soon, so the bank can't use it to make money, and thus, they don't pay for the privilege of holding on to this money.

Overdraft Fees—

The last piece to cover here is overdraft fees for insufficient funds. They are real, and yes, you will implement them. The first time your daughter writes a check and she doesn't have the money to cover it, you will accept the check, put her checking account into the negative for the item purchased and then add a $30 insufficient funds fee to her account. Never let your daughter write two "bad checks" in a row, however. We are not training criminals, here. The second time she attempts to write a check when she doesn't have the money in her account . . . decline it. The first instance is on her, along with the $30 insufficient funds fee; the second time, you step in. Also, take notes on the incident because the next Weekly Meeting definitely has to cover why it's not okay to write checks when she doesn't have the money in her account. The fee might seem harsh, but it's realistic and hopefully it's a lesson she will only have to learn once.

Chapter 8

Automatic Teller Machines (ATM)

The next section dealing with money management is the automated teller machine or ATM. The Family Bank ATM is always available, but, of course, there is a $3 dollar fee. Wait until little Mr. Reckless masters the use of his checking and savings account before you explain what an ATM is and how it works. Kids have a tendency to want to hold on to cash, so kids that are too young will abuse the ATM and not understand why you are "stealing" their money every time they make an ATM withdrawal. A misunderstanding like this will cause your son to resent your Family Bank, so we don't want to throw ATM's into the mix until he is old enough to understand the cause and effect of paying a fee to withdraw cash. When your son understands the function and the necessity of ATM's, and after some minor ATM abuses, you'll be able to show him how much money he has lost in ATM fees and how to avoid them. One method could be by using his debit card at the grocery store to purchase something he needs and taking an extra $20 dollars in cash out at that time.

This covers the savings, checking and ATM sections and getting your Family Bank up and running. However, we didn't cover lesson plans for every single Weekly Meeting. It will be up to you to come up with your own lessons between all the main points of The Family Bank. You know, all those meetings in between opening his savings account, opening his checking account and getting his ATM card. Just teach him what you know. Focus on teaching him how to keep his notebook in order and field all his questions about what banks are and how they work. Teach him what a check is and how it works, how a debit card is just a more convenient version of a check, what an ATM is and how it works, and what ATM and overdraft fees are.

During these Weekly Meetings, also talk to him about why it's important to save money; for example, so he can buy people presents when he needs to and buy himself new clothes when necessary. At this age, children don't comprehend or care about saving for retirement or college, so make the idea of saving money tangible and "short term" and something he cares about, like saving up to buy a new bike in the spring. After all, learning how to save money is really about learning how to control the impulse to spend money, and if Mr. Reckless learns to save for a bike today, then it will be much easier for him to save for college tomorrow.

Finally, for my favorite Weekly Meetings . . . field trips. The weekend after I show my daughter a new aspect of The Family Bank, I make that Weekly Meeting a field trip. Field Trips are important, because not only do we get some quality time together, but I get to show her how the things she just learned about work in real life: be it a check, a debit card, an ATM or an ATM fee! So, take her to the mall, go up to an ATM and show her how you put in your code and withdraw money, and show her where it tells you it is going to subtract a fee from your account. Then show her the receipt after it prints. You take these things for granted, but kids are amazed to see things they just learned being used in real life.

SECTION III

Family Bank Employment

The Family Bank is full of lessons to teach your kids, and so far we have only skimmed the surface. In the next few sections, we will cover topics such as how to manage credit cards, apply for loans, and also how your daughter will start her own business. However, before we can get into those topics, we have to cover the topic of Family Bank Employment. This next section is "Employment", because The Family Bank and Financial System makes the most sense when we cover all the topics of the book in the same order that you will implement them with your children. So, before we delve into credit, your bank member needs to have a job! That's right, employment. *You* can't get credit without being able to show income and assets, so neither will your son or daughter.

Chapter 9

Searching for Employment

Setting Up—

Where do people go to look for work? We used to look in the newspaper, ask friends and family and go to college job fairs. But now, more and more, we use the Internet to search for jobs that meet our qualifications and post resumes online. As nice as it would be to be able to teach our kids the perfect place to go to find the perfect job, there just isn't one special place to look that is going to have the perfect job for everyone. Therefore, teaching your kids where to go to look for employment is up to you, so do the best you can. Everyone who reads The Family Bank will have different contacts, levels of education and live in vastly different locations, so although the principles covered in this book are universal, where your kids can go to look for employment really doesn't have a universal answer. In order to keep this book useful to everyone, I am going to bypass where to look for a real job, and leave that section up to you to determine and incorporate into your Family Bank. What we will talk about, though, is the general employment process and getting a job as part of The Family Bank and Financial System.

It is important to implement employment into your Financial System as early as possible, but after your kids have really mastered the concept of a savings account, checking account, checks and their ATM debit card. If you start The Family Bank when your son is eight years old, then I would wait until he is about nine years old to introduce him to the "job hunt". Of course, if your child is 12 years old right now and already has a general understanding of savings and checking accounts, then you can follow up with employment about a month or so after you start up your family bank. If your kids are a little older, then you must be prepared for, "okayyyyy . . . D-a-d . . . I'm not stupid. I understand what a checking account is!" Don't let this minor resistance discourage you and don't skip sections of The Family Bank because you think your child already understands them. Even if your daughter is fifteen years old and already has a solid foundation, she still won't be used to using a checking account through The Family Bank, and with the special rules The Family Bank has in place (like giving a check to you in order to purchase an item). So let your child become proficient with The Family Bank before you introduce Family Bank Employment.

Creating The Family Bank is vitally important in the long run, and once it's running your kids will appreciate the organization it brings to their financial lives. Also, don't let your kids rush you. You have ample time. The idea is to get them through every level of your financial system before they leave the nest, not before the end of the week. So, even if your kids are a little older and understand some of the basics about mechanically controlling and moving their money, let the concept of The Family Bank sink in a little before you introduce them to Employment and The Family Financial System. The Family Bank is a proverbial "marathon, not a sprint", so don't feel the need to rush through every section of The Family Bank.

All you will physically need to add to your Family Bank to begin incorporating employment is a cork board on the wall next to your whiteboard. The cork board is where you will post employment opportunities. Literally, all you will have to do is print or hand write a flyer with all the job information on it and tack it to the cork board. It's a little old fashioned, but it gets the job done. On the other hand, if you'd rather create your own website and post your Family Bank job listings there, and have your daughter submit her resume to you online too, then that's great! That's a little too over the top for most of us, though, so I'm not going to go into detail about how to make this section of The Family Bank web-based. I will limit my discussion of job listing to the trusty cork board.

Responsibility—

A job is a huge responsibility . . . shocker, huh? With this in mind, you will treat your employees EXACTLY the same whether they are nine years old or sixteen years old. How is that possible? It's all about the amount of responsibility their job requires. Did you ask your parents for a dog when you were seven years old, and hear, "only if you promise to take care of it", or something to that effect? The problem with that is that first, being responsible for a living being is too great a responsibility for a seven-year-old, and second, you have no recourse if your son stops taking care of his dog. In the end, the dog has to be cared for, so you will be forced to do his job for him, thus teaching your son that if he is not responsible, other people will cover for him. Therefore, with too great a responsibility too early, you are both set up for failure from the beginning.

A job that a nine-year-old can handle might be picking up and putting away all the toys in the house, to include her room, five days a week. It's a job she can do and it's a job you can let slide for a day if she stops doing it, unlike feeding the dog. Remember, you are the boss, so you set the rules. Just keep in mind that the objective of your child's first job is to endow her with just enough responsibility that she will be successful, but also get a feel for the "daily grind" and how to push through it.

The Want Ads—

Let's say that Little Miss Thrifty is nine years old and has had a checking and savings account for about a year, now. She has been saving every penny she gets from her grandparents and she has also put all her birthday money straight into savings, but as the holidays draw near you explain to her (during your Weekly Meeting) that people have a social obligation to buy each other presents during these special times of the year, and, of course, that it's always better to give than to receive! So the holidays, falling right after "back to school", will inevitably wipe out Miss Thrifty's savings and checking accounts, which is exactly what you will have been hoping for! Miss Thrifty is starting to feel pressure, because she is beginning to realize that she is spending more money than she is bringing in. She's also realizing, of course, that on top of her obligations, there are also things she wants, like new designer boots. Miss Thrifty is starting to feel the pressure of wanting stuff that she does not have the money to buy.

About this time is when you are thinking that her toys are always all over the floor, even though you've been telling her to pick them up every day for the past . . . oh, nine years now. So it's time to sit down and post your first job opening. You can either design a job listing on your computer or hand write it. You will need to include the following: job title, position level, general duties, hours, salary and benefits (no hourly wages, we're not rewarding them for moving as slowly as humanly possible) and method of contact. After you've written up your job posting, just tack it to your cork board. For example:

WANTED
Toy Cleanup Specialist
Entry level
Responsibilities include:
Clean up all the toys in the house to include your bedroom

Thursday-Monday
24 days of vacation per year, 12 sick days per year
3 dollars per week
Apply in person

The actual title of the position you create is inconsequential, but the fact that the job has a title is important. Just having a title changes the work itself from a series of menial tasks into a job. Having a title adds a feeling of duty and responsibility. It's much easier to quit taking out the garbage after dinner than it is to quit a job as a Kitchen Sanitation Assistant.

I also mentioned different levels of employment within The Family Bank. As your child gets older and more mature, and as his financial needs increase, so must his responsibility and pay increase. The Family Bank and Financial System utilizes five levels of employment: Entry Level, Associate, Lower Management, Mid-Level Management and Executive. I hesitate to assign dollar amounts to these positions in this book, because different family budgets are going to allow for different salary ranges at each level. Just make the salaries you assign to each level realistic for both your child and your budget. Most important, though, is that each level of employment maintains its own unique level of responsibility. Each level of responsibility will not necessarily translate directly to certain age groups, but I'll give you some general age ranges and you can determine what works for you and your family.

- Entry level employment is for the first year of Family Bank employment, nine to ten years old ideally, and should consist of only a single task like taking out all the garbage in the house or putting away all the toys in the house. Also, the task should not take longer than 5 to 10 minutes to complete.

- Associate level employment should begin to feel like a real job, and works well for kids around the ten—to eleven-year-old range. We are increasing the responsibility level slowly, so two small tasks are ideal here; for example, clearing the table and loading the dishwasher, or vacuuming and dusting the living room in your house.

- Low Level Management, the eleven—to twelve-year-old range, is the first employment section that should seem more like a real job. This level is management, so you want your kids to have to manage their time and the quality of their work. A Low Level Management position is one that requires the completion of a large task, which should take somewhere in the 20 to 30 minute range to complete. An example would be lawn care, which might consist of both mowing and edging once a week, and pulling weeds three days per week. This job requires your daughter to manage both her time and her resources (such as keeping enough fuel for the mower on hand) and also requires that she maintain a certain standard of quality, unlike a job such as taking out the garbage, which is either done or not done. Another example would be cleaning the bathroom, which is a several step process, with easily recognizable standards of quality.

- Mid-Level Management is designed for the twelve—to fourteen-year-old age range. Mid-Level Management should consist of two large tasks, which can either be related (help cook dinner and then clean up after dinner), or they can be unrelated (clean the bathroom and mow the lawn).

- Executive positions are the cream of the crop jobs and they are what you want your child to strive to obtain. These jobs pay very well, require a high level of responsibility and self-motivation, and are reserved for those applicants with at least three years of related experience. Yes, we're talking about a long-term commitment here. Executive positions include Head Chef, Groundskeeper, Event Planner, or whatever you can imagine. Later in the book, we will discuss bills your child will have to pay to you, to include renting his bedroom from you for around $400 per month. So, the Executive level positions should offer a monthly salary in the $500 to $600 range (again, keep in mind that 90%-95% of that money will be coming back to you in the form of bills your kids pay to you). For an Executive level position example, let's take a look at Head Chef. The Head Chef is in charge of keeping an inventory of the food and ingredients in the kitchen, creating a menu of all the dinners (and the ingredients required) for the work week, which he will get approved and have turned in to you 2 weeks in advance (so you can add them to your shopping list), and he will be in charge of all of the dinner preparation and clean up. You can see that Executive level jobs require a great deal of time and energy, but also pay well and prepare your child for the duties, expectations and responsibilities of the real world.

We've discussed job titles and position levels, so next is the job description. A couple key points to expand upon here: your listing must be specific and it must be all inclusive. Specific and all inclusive means you can't write, "clean up all the toys in the house to include your bedroom and *other chores as needed*". Although many real jobs have these types of general descriptions, your nine-year-old's first job must be clearly spelled out. When your kids get older and they begin applying for Mid-Level or Executive positions you will be able to add general descriptions such as: maintain order and cleanliness of entire house, or special duties include party planning and decorating, as required. In the beginning, during the Entry Level positions, the concept of having a job is going to be difficult for a child to understand and he will tire of it quickly, so you'll have to keep it very simple. Learning to cope with the responsibility of a job is a long-term process, so no matter how excited you are to hand over the reins of the kitchen, be prepared to take the Family Employment section slowly.

As you both become more comfortable with The Family Bank and Financial System, the level of responsibility will be continuously evolving to suit your child's needs. In addition to keeping the duties simple and direct, everything listed in this first job posting is non negotiable. I would actually be quite surprised if your nine-year-old does try to negotiate with you! Later on, though, mid-level and executive level positions will have vague descriptions and you can introduce your son or daughter to salary and benefits negotiation, but all entry level positions must be clear, direct and non-negotiable.

Now that we've ventured into the realm of employment within The Family Financial System, let's explore where we can go with this. You started your job listing with one single job posting in order to keep things simple, but, of course, you have a lot of options and room to grow right along with your kids. The driving force behind The Family Bank is your children, so as their needs change, so must the products offered by your bank. When $5 a week is no longer enough to sustain the lifestyle your daughter is living, whether it's due to her wanting new clothes or to you beginning to charge her for rent and food, eventually your daughter is going to need a higher paying job. Perfect, because you are getting tired of vacuuming, washing the car and mowing the lawn, anyway! At this point it's time to expand the job listings with some more options.

Once The Family Bank is put into effect, your bank members are completely on their own when it comes to making money and purchasing items they need. The only exception to this rule is if you implement The Family Bank early, when your son turns seven or eight. If you are starting The Family Bank with your eight-year-old you will have to transition from buying everything for him, to him buying what he needs for himself. Once you make this transition, or if you start The Family Bank with a child older than eight, you will no longer buy him clothes, shoes, school supplies, toys, presents for his family members, etc. You will, however, still buy him birthday presents and take him out to dinner or for ice cream and things like that, but no more "freebie" shopping. "Freebie" shopping is any shopping like buying him a remote control car just because he really wants it and he doesn't have the money to buy it himself. I can't stress the point enough that The Family Bank will not function properly if you continue to do *any* freebie shopping for your kids. By creating this dynamic, where he can't get handouts, he will be forced to learn how to think ahead, manage his money and with your help, in a Weekly Meeting, create a budget. If your concern here is that he may have to go without new clothes, so be it. If your concern is that he will miss out on something he actually needs, like cleats for football season, well that is why we will cover loans and credit in later chapters. All his needs will be met, but just like you (as an Adult), he will be responsible for how his needs get met!

Let's say your ten-year-old daughter now needs to make $20 a week in order to be able to afford the things she needs and to have a little money left over for the things she wants. You're probably thinking, "That's outrageous! I could never afford $80 per month!" Although $20 per week might sound like a lot, especially if you're comparing it to how much "allowance" you used to receive as a child, $1040 a year is probably much less than you would spend if you were keeping track of everything you currently buy for her. Her salary has to cover not only the bills you are going to charge her, but also new clothes, new shoes, school supplies, birthday presents for various relatives, and hopefully an occasional item that she wants to buy for herself, like maybe that mp3 player that you would otherwise have ended up buying for her.

It's important not to compare your daughter's wages to the allowance you had growing up. You are teaching your kids how to handle money by letting them actually handle their own money; in fact, they are just handling for themselves all the money that you would have been spending on them anyway. I know; tricky, right? Growing up, your allowance was money "in your pocket" that you could spend; but your daughter has bills to pay, so don't be afraid to pay her what she needs in order to survive.

Now that we're on the same page again, let's get back to creating some job postings after your daughter has been employed for a while. You'll sit down and create maybe three listings for jobs that all pay $20 per week (Associate) and one listing for a job that pays $35 per week (Low-Level Management). The Low-Level Management position will look very tempting to your daughter, but it will have a requirement of experience in an "Associate" level position. Let your daughter apply for this Low-Level Management job, if that is what she wants. Even encourage her to apply for it, but make sure you explain to her, in a Weekly Meeting before she applies, that she is not yet qualified for the Low-Level Management position. If she does apply, then during the interview you will have to ask her really tough questions, such as "tell me about your experiences in the Associate level position" and "what makes you qualified to handle this position?" Of course, if she applies for the Low-Level Management position, you won't be able to hire her due to her lack of professional experience, but the extra practice with interviewing is still valuable and she'll learn the lesson that adults don't get anything, especially good jobs, for free. Adults have to work hard and work their way up. During the Weekly Meeting after her Low-Level Management position interview, you will need to sit down with her and create a career track to help her obtain the necessary experience to be able to land that Low-Level Management position in the future. But I digress, and we will cover the interview process in a later chapter.

Don't shy away from seasonal employment by trying to make a job last all year, or by creating a list of tasks that change by season: Mow the lawn and pull weeds (May through September), rake leaves (October through November), shovel snow (December through February), and wash the car (March through April). You can see that the list is tedious and the weather will never cooperate with your designated dates; you'll end up giving her months off at a time. Allow yourself to post seasonal employment. For example: Mow the lawn and pull weeds (May through the end of the season). By building in a definite, yet unknown end date, your daughter will have to plan to apply and interview for a new job before the end of the season, in order to have continuing employment. This is a lesson I happened to learn personally by doing seasonal work on a golf course for three years during high school. The added planning and budgeting is a bonus, not a problem.

The only really big considerations while creating these positions are that the amount of work and responsibility are proportionate to the pay and benefits, and that they are all in line with your son's age. Remember the example of giving a dog to a seven-year-old? The positions you create for your son should incorporate his interests, compensate him fairly and not require more responsibility than he can handle. Don't be surprised, when you first mention the idea of Family Bank employment to your son, for him to jump all over it and be incredibly excited. He'll probably start listing numerous chores that he can do and asking you how much money he'll get for each one. After you introduce him to the idea of a Family Bank job, just tell him to be patient and start watching the cork board for job postings. Then start small. Even if junior knows how to do the entire after-dinner cleanup and wants that to be his job, that doesn't mean it would be a good first job for him.

Kids get bored and distracted easily and it's imperative that once your son starts his Family Bank and Financial System employment that, by no means, does it EVER fall by the wayside. You cannot get to the point where you both just give up on it and forget about it. When he gets tired of his new job after one week and wants to quit, you cannot, under any circumstances, just let the responsibility of his employment fade away without consequences. Don't be lazy, here. It is for both his long-term benefit and yours that you follow the guidelines laid out here and continue plugging away at the The Family Bank employment system. Just remember: keep his first job simple, very simple.

Employment is going to be the longest running and arguably the most complicated aspect of The Family Bank Financial system. The jobs have to get more complex and the pay has to get better. You'll have to offer different employment options and tailor them to fit your child and you'll have to deal with write-ups for missed work days, bonuses and promotions. Having said that, don't be overwhelmed. You have ten years, give or take, to figure it all out, and once you get started you will get a feel for how your kids handle employment and your role will become self-explanatory. Remember, your son's first job will be something along the lines of taking the garbage out each night after dinner for three dollars per week. You can handle that, I promise. Employment is the most important, most interesting and most rewarding part of The Family Bank Financial System for you and for your kids, so have fun with it.

Chapter 10

Building a Resume

If teaching your son that he has to find a job and showing him where to look for one is the first step in Family Bank Employment, then teaching your son how to create a resume and how to apply for a job is the next step. Different resume formats abound and we are not going to cover them all in this book. For simplicity's sake, I am going to use a clean, generic version of a resume that is modeled after the Microsoft Elegant Resume template. This section is about getting your child familiar with the concept of creating a resume, the content of each of the major sections found on most resumes, and the idea that he has to create a separate, targeted resume for each and every job to which he applies. Therefore, use whichever template you are the most comfortable with, just make sure it is simple.

So now that you've got the concept of employment within The Family Financial System down, it's time to get the ball rolling. After you create that first job posting, you are going to have to explain the employment process to your son at the next Weekly Meeting. Explain to him that because you don't give him an allowance, and because his needs keep increasing, he will need to find a way to make money on his own. Keeping in mind that your son is around nine years old, show him the job posting you created and ask him if he is interested in applying for that position. If he says no, don't push him; a negative response means he's not ready yet. Sooner rather than later, though, he is going to want something, like a video game. These desires serve as great lead-ins to remind him that he can always apply to that job posted at The Family Bank.

Eventually, your son is going to come around and ask you how to apply for a job with the Family Bank. Take this opportunity to teach him the job application process, starting with how to build a resume. Sit with him during your next Weekly Meeting and show him your resume, which he is not going to understand, and help him to start building his own. Most word processing programs come with generic resume builders, so open up your favorite and use the simplest one you can find, or even hand write one. Help him fill in his name, address, phone number and email if he has it, in the header at the top of the page. Then move along to actual resume sections: Objective, Prior Employment History, Extracurricular Experience (Activities), Special Skills, and Education and References.

What you might not realize is that these sections of a resume are simple and straightforward to complete, yet most people struggle with building a resume because they don't see a real resume until they are in their 20's! Not being introduced to a resume until your son is in his 20's is absurd! How will he know what skills he needs to be developing in school and in life, if he doesn't see how those skills impact his resume until after he has finished college? Well, you are going to use the Family

Bank to compensate for this knowledge gap by covering each of the most common sections of a resume with your son. Keep in mind, though, that you can spread these lessons out over a few Weekly Meetings if you want, because a nine-year-old will not be able to absorb everything you have to teach him in one Weekly Meeting.

Objective—

First is the Objective section. The Objective section is very short. If your son is submitting a resume for a job opening as an Associate Custodian, then the Objective section will say, Objective: Obtain employment as Associate Custodian. Later on, in the "real world", resumes will also be submitted with applications for promotions or lateral assignments, in which case the Objective section will be tailored to that specific posting.

Employment History—

Second is Employment History, which in this case will be very, very short, but growing with every job your son successfully obtains and maintains. Each of your son's previous employment experiences will go in this section. This will build a work history that his future employers can analyze, to gain perspective of his overall experience and qualifications.

On a side note, have your son choose his ideal career and write it down on a separate sheet of paper or in his notebook (like a Doctor or even a Professional Football Player). Help your son to focus on obtaining Family Bank jobs that aid him in building an employment experience base that will qualify him for his future "dream" career. If your son wants to become a doctor, then it is important to find a job that requires a high level of attention to detail. A possible first job could be straightening up and organizing his toys or hand washing the dishes in the evening. These are jobs that require a sense of orderliness and attention to detail, all good traits to develop early in a budding doctor.

Also, don't worry that his career will change every six months. Just keep coming up with employment that fits along his general career path. If he wants to play football, let him focus on manual labor like cutting grass, raking leaves or shoveling snow, etc. It's pretty simple if you think about it. Once your son gets a few different jobs under his belt, show him how each job, listed sequentially in the employment section, paints a picture of his overall work experience for his perspective employer. Your son's "dream career" will change many times as he grows up, which is good; just always be teaching him how to manipulate the "Previous Employment" section of his resume to help him apply for his newest job interest. As your son changes career paths, show him how to highlight the skills he's learned from his previous jobs, which show development toward this new "ideal" career path.

In order to tailor each job on his resume for a specific job posting, you will show him how to change the "bullets" that explain his achievements, and show him how to highlight different achievements for each career he is considering. If your son wants to be a Basketball player and has been taking out the garbage for the past six months, he could write: threw the garbage bag into the trash can 120 times and never missed the can; or, if he wants to be a doctor: collected and disposed of all household garbage 120 times with zero spills or accidents. Teach your son to list his previous employment in a manner that highlights his achievements and demonstrates experience in a specific career path progression.

Extracurricular Experience (Activities)—

Third is Extracurricular Experience (Activities). This section is where the bulk of this first resume and most of his future resumes are going to be generated. These activities can include: volunteer work (or volunteer chores), sports, hobbies and/or anything you can think of that is somehow representative of your child's unique, non work-related experience. As your son gets older and you begin to help him generate different resumes for different employment opportunities, help him focus on adding only the extracurricular activities that show skills or personality traits that are in-line with the position to which he is applying. Playing recreation league basketball is pertinent to applying for a basketball coaching position for his younger sister, but typing 60 words per minute really isn't relevant unless the position requires that he write progress reports.

Extracurricular Experience is a broad category, and this happens to bring us to an area of tremendous potential. Most kids don't like to do volunteer work, and I'm not adding volunteer work as a mandatory part of The Family Bank Financial System, but hear me out for a moment . . . You've already set the stage, because your son has a blank page in front of him that he knows he has to fill in order to create a truly impressive resume. Like a video game, he is going to want to rack up the points in order to have the best resume. He also has an understanding that Extracurricular Experiences help to land jobs, especially when his work experience is sparse. Couple this with the fact that he wants to be a doctor when he grows up, and why not take him every other weekend for a couple months to volunteer to visit with the elderly at the local nursing home? This would fill four Weekly Meeting slots, give him some volunteer time to add to his resume and also give him a real life look at what it's like to be around people who need a lot of medical attention. You don't have to make long-term volunteering commitments; even volunteering only once or twice can be very meaningful. The more volunteer work he does, though, the more long-term "real life" benefits he will obtain.

When your son is applying for college or for his first job after college, often the only distinguishing factor between hundreds of applicants with similar academic records is volunteer work. Not to mention the character growth that comes from volunteering. Anyway, enough said on volunteer work; it's a good idea to incorporate it as much as it is reasonable for your family and for your family's schedule. The benefits for you, your kids and the people your son will end up helping is immeasurable. So, help your son to fill in that gap on his resume known as "Extracurricular Experience (Activities)". Volunteer work is just one idea, though. You can teach him to fill that space with any number of activities: drawing, horseback riding, playing the piano, clubs, sports, church groups or anything else in which he is involved.

Special Skills—

The fourth section of your son's resume is Special Skills. Special Skills are any skills your son has obtained that are not common to the average job applicant. Some Special Skills include: typing, familiarity with basic computer programs like Excel and PowerPoint, speaking a second language, sewing, playing the piano, drawing, horseback riding or any other special skills you can imagine. When I was thirteen years old, I learned how to make Medieval Chainmail armor at summer camp. Making Chainmail could definitely be listed in the Special Skills section of my resume, if I were applying for a job that involved any kind of organizational skills or required attention to detail. Most skills are self-explanatory and you can encourage your son to try to master skills of his choosing in his free time. Typing, for example, is always a beneficial skill and is one that your child can easily master in his or her free time. He can play free online typing games on the family's computer or take a typing class in high school. If I had had this phenomenal advice and taken such a class, you could have read this book six months ago!

Education—

The fifth section we will touch on is Education. In this section, have your child list the highest grade level completed and any special classes he has taken. Although typical high school and college classes are never listed in the Education section of a real resume, technical or trade schools can be listed here. Get him used to thinking about the totality of his education and being able to articulate it in his resume. The education section of a real resume is reserved for educational experiences in which a person acquires some sort of degree or diploma, but for The Family Bank you will treat any kind of "certificate of completion" as a an official diploma and list the class in the Education section.

While I was growing up I took an Electronics class and received a certificate for it. I also took wood shop and home economics, like everyone else, but I didn't receive anything special for those classes. When your son takes elective classes and he doesn't receive a certificate for them, print (or hand write) one at home and give it to him. Have your son list these classes under Education, because it teaches him to think in terms of what he has learned that is relevant to the job for which he is applying; and more importantly, when an opportunity arises to take a class that he knows he can add to his resume, he will be more likely to sign up for it and take advantage of that opportunity.

A word of caution here: be careful not to list the same information in different sections, unless his resume is really sparse. For example, if your son takes a typing class and graduates with a Certificate of Completion, he might be tempted to list the typing class in his Education section, and "type 60 words per minute" in the Special Skills section. Only put the information in the section where it looks more impressive. In this case, listing "type 60 words per minute" in the Special Skills section is more impressive than listing the class itself in the Education section. However, if a class does not lead to a specific skill, like taking Advanced Algebra over the summer, then list the course with dates attended and the certificate obtained in the Education section.

References—

The final section is the References section. References are not usually included on a resume; however, starting to think about them and understanding the importance of good references is so important that you should add a references section to your child's resume. Remember, the real lessons of the resume section of The Family Bank Financial

System are to teach your child that resumes exist, that a new resume is created specifically for each job listing and that the function of a good resume is to give a clear picture of all his experience.

References are usually included in the application for employment, but I have not included an application for employment as part of The Family Bank Financial System. An actual application for employment ends up being too labor intensive for you. Creating an application for employment is tedious and you are basically going to have to fill out the application yourself while you explain every detail to your nine-year-old. Just trust me that for simplicity's sake it is better to forgo the job application and make sure your son has a solid grasp of the business resume. The resume is the most important teaching tool in this section and you don't want it to be thought of as another annoying piece of paperwork that your son has to rush through to get to what's important, which in his mind will be starting his new job. This is not to say that you can't include applications for employment, I just haven't done it here. But, if you do include them, be sure they don't interfere with the resume building process.

Let's get back to References. When it comes to implementing reference checks into the employment hiring process, keep in mind the only references he will have will be you, and possibly any other "head of household" who is Co-CEO of The Family Bank with you. These references are going to help you add a layer of accountability to your son's work ethic. The first time he goes to apply for a better job and you explain that you won't hire him, because his reference said he was often late for work and his work ethic is questionable, he will see how his past performance holds him accountable. At your next Weekly

Meeting, you'll have to explain that he will have to continue at his current position for two more months, be on time to work every day and be an ideal employee, in order to change his bosses' perception of him. After he gets a couple good performance reviews, he will be able to reapply for the new position with a positive referral from his boss.

Having references will illustrate to your son that keeping a good work record is important. He will not be able to get a good reference from his "old boss" if he was unreliable or performed his job poorly. We will discuss work performance and how it affects future employment potential in a later chapter, but obviously if he gets fired from his position as Associate Custodian and is no longer collecting a paycheck every week, he will quickly understand how important it is to stay in good standing at work. Also, once he gets fired from a job, the next job he applies for will have to be another low level job, because he won't have any references to help him get a higher level job. Good references are vital to successfully obtaining employment, so we definitely want to drive that point home.

Learning how to build a strong resume is imperative in today's workforce. Children are never taught this skill in school, so all too often they end up turning in weak resumes or paying hundreds of dollars each time they need to have someone else do it for them. The key to a strong resume is to keep it simple. I have had a lot of success in my life getting interviews based on the resumes that I have turned in and the reason is simple: literally. No professional resume should ever be longer than two pages no matter how much experience has to be crammed into it. Also, make the resume visually appealing, simple and to the point.

The final step to ensuring your son has a good resume is to hand it to someone who is either busy or lazy, and ask her what she likes about it. If she glances at it and says, "It's easy to read and get the pertinent information quickly", then he has a good resume. If she hands it back to him and says, "I don't have the time to look at it now", then the problem is the resume, not her schedule; he needs to make it simpler. His audience should be able to glean all the pertinent information from his resume in about the same amount of time it would take to say, "I don't have time to look at it right now." If your son hears that magic phrase, then it's "back to the drawing board".

There are literally hundreds of resume formats out there, if you do an Internet search for "resume templates". I recommend doing this search, but make sure that when you glance at the template you ask yourself how the template looks. If it seems too busy or the pertinent information doesn't jump out at you, then move on to the next one. My "go to" resume format is the Microsoft Office Elegant Resume.

If you are reflecting on this section of The Family Bank Financial System and thinking, "I don't have the time or the desire to read through a bunch of resumes", then you truly understand what the Human Resources Manager will be thinking when your son will someday hand her his resume. Now do what you've got to do; take that knowledge and pass it along to your child.

Chapter 11

Preparing for the Interview

Now that your daughter has mastered the basics of The Family Bank and realized that she needs more money, you have introduced her to the prospect of Family Bank employment. You posted a job, or maybe a few, to the cork board, and she expressed interest in obtaining said employment. You then explained the hiring process to her during a Weekly Meeting and helped her build her resume, which she turned in to your Family Bank inbox. She is now eagerly awaiting a callback. So you call her on the phone, introduce yourself as Mr. (your last name) and set up an interview time. Tell her that you thought her resume was very impressive and you'd like to interview her at the office of The Family Bank at "such and such" time, and the interview will be a Standard Interview (or a Behavioral Interview, if it's not her first interview, but more on this topic to follow). Well, now that the callback is out of the way, what next?

The interview time you set up has to be far enough out that you give yourself enough time to prepare for the interview, so allow for at LEAST one Weekly Meeting before the interview. If it's her first job interview, then I would allow three or four weeks before the interview. The interview process is always a formal process and you want to increase the tension surrounding this process as much as possible. What good does it do if you both show up in your pajamas and you hire her on the spot? Every section of The Family Bank is a learning tool and this is no exception. The job interview is my favorite section of The Family Bank, because this is where you get to see your little nine-year-old all dressed up and acting professional.

At the first Weekly Meeting after scheduling the job interview, you have to explain the interview process and subsequent hiring process. Keep in mind, there are graduate level college courses on this material, but I am going to keep it very simple here, because you are introducing this process to a nine-year-old. Explain to her that an interview is a formal process, wherein her potential employer will ask her a series of questions. The questions are meant to reveal what type of person she is, how well she works with other people, if she is the type of person who will take her job seriously and if she'll be a hard worker. Once the interviewers have finished asking her all their questions, they will give her a chance to ask them questions. Then the interview will be over. Before the interview even starts, though, the person asking her the questions will have looked over her resume in order to learn a little bit about her, where she is coming from and how much experience she has working in the field for which she is applying.

Weekly Meeting 1—Standard Interview versus Behavioral Interview—

This first Weekly Meeting, before the interview, is when you will explain that there are a few different types of interviews. The two types of interviews you will cover are what are commonly referred to as the Standard Interview and the Behavioral Interview. When you interview your daughter you will use the Standard Interview process until you think she is old enough and mature enough to understand and prepare for a Behavioral Interview; no sooner than twelve years old. Between nine and twelve years old, don't focus too much on explaining the Behavioral Interview; just make her aware that it exists. Only delve into the Behavioral Interview explanation and preparation process when your daughter applies for Mid-level or Executive level employment.

Standard Interview—

Patiently explain that during a Standard Interview the interviewer will ask her to give some personal background and then ask her generic questions like, "what is your greatest strength?", "what is your greatest weakness?" or "why do you believe you will succeed in this position?", etc. All the questions in Standard Interviews are generic and hypothetical. When your daughter answers Standard Interview questions she will have to generate truthful answers that make her look hard working and responsible. For example, she could be asked a question like, "How would you handle a confrontation with your boss?" This question is hypothetical and your daughter will have to respond with a hypothetical answer, such as, "I would explain my position thoroughly, but in the end I would do what my boss wants me to do, as long as it is legal."

When your daughter gets to higher level positions, then you'll explain the Behavioral Interview. The Behavioral Interview is not generic or hypothetical and it's becoming very popular in the business world today, which means your kids are going to face a different gauntlet of interview questions than you did in your day. She may get a lead-in like, "Tell me about yourself," but the rest of the questions are specific and refer to a specific experience in her life. For example, "Tell me about a time you had a conflict with your boss and how you resolved that conflict," or "Tell me about your greatest achievement at your last job." As you notice, the questions are really statements that require truthful answers based on prior experience. A Behavioral Interview is always formal, is often timed and is extremely rigid.

Behavioral Interview answers are equally as formal as the questions. When your daughter answers Behavioral Interview questions the answers must be three part answers, explaining *the situation she was in, what she did in that situation and the outcome of her action.* Utilizing this three part answer is absolutely vital to doing well in a Behavioral Interview.

During these pre-interview Weekly Meetings you will stress to your daughter that the objective of the interview process is to make herself come across sounding as intelligent and responsible as possible, by putting thought into every answer. If she is facing a Behavioral Interview, let her know in the Weekly Meeting that there are a limited number of Behavioral Interview questions and that an Internet search will quickly reveal them. Also, inform her that the proper way to prepare for a Behavioral Interview is to set aside some personal time during the week and to sit and think about each question, then write out a paragraph for each type of question that is based on a time in her life. Behavioral Interviews draw questions from a small and limited pool; about ten to fifteen different categories (depending on who you ask), but there are many ways to phrase similar questions within each category. Thinking up about ten to fifteen different scenarios will usually cover every type of question. Ten scenarios is the magic number here. If your daughter writes out too many scenarios, then she won't be able to remember them all during the interview.

This book is not a "how-to guide" to successful interviewing techniques, as that topic would be an entire book in itself. You may not have faced each type of interview, however. Therefore, I will outline an example from a Behavioral Interview, so you will know you're on the right track. Some of the general categories of questions include: Problem Solving Skills, Communication, Decision Making Ability, Initiative, Integrity, Leadership, and Teamwork. Your daughter might face a question like, "Tell me about a time when you faced a moral dilemma in your life and how you resolved that situation." Remember that within a category there will be a slew of questions, but most of the questions will be driving at the same point and she is not likely to encounter more than one or two questions from any given category during an interview.

Have your daughter sit down before the interview, research the different categories, think about a time either personally or professionally (home life, school, Family Bank job, after school activities, etc.) that relates to each category of questions and have her write out a one paragraph answer, based on her personal experience, for each category. She won't be able to take the written paragraphs into the interview, so she'll have to read over what she wrote a few times and become thoroughly familiar with her answers. She can't memorize them, though, because when the questions come during the interview they will not be exactly the same as the ones she used to write her paragraph, so she will have to finagle each answer on the spot. Sounds complicated, doesn't it? That's why it's so incredibly important for you to teach these lessons to your children while they are young, before she ends up in the hot seat completely unprepared for the interview that could land her that dream job.

During a successful Behavioral Interview, your daughter will have to give the interviewer a well-rounded glimpse of her whole life, not just her work-related experience. She should create different scenarios from every aspect of her life: an accomplishment from Girl Scouts (personal achievement), a conflict with a family member (conflict resolution), a large project she finished in school (time management), a situation in her first job when she was asked to forge paperwork (ethical dilemma), etc. By developing answers to each Behavioral Interview section from all the different aspects of her life, she will give the interviewer a well-rounded look at herself as a person, highlighting all her achievements and also answering all the Behavioral Interview questions in exactly the way the interviewer wants.

Sound like all this is getting too complicated and too unfamiliar? That is precisely the reason you are running The Family Bank. Imagine yourself walking into an interview at 20 years old and having never been exposed to a Behavioral Interview by anyone at school or at home . . . it's a lot like getting hit by a bus, a stress bus. It's your job as a loving and responsible parent to use The Family Bank to prepare your children for this special treat. Do your homework, which will take you about ten minutes to run an Internet search for Standard Interviews and Behavioral Interviews, and run your twelve-year-old through the wringer. You'll both learn from the experience and by the time your daughter has run through her fifth Behavioral Interview with you, you will both be experts and she will have a **monumental** advantage over all the other applicants at her first real job interview. I promise that the extra effort you put in here will be well worth it in the long run, and your daughter will thank you immensely when it's finally "show time".

Keep in mind that while your daughter is young, you will focus on Standard Interviews only. During the Weekly Meetings for her very first job interview, don't worry about making her understand the details of the Behavioral Interview; focus your energy on helping her prepare for a Standard Interview. Do some quick research online for Standard Interview questions and let her know during this meeting what types of questions she will be facing. Basically, the types of questions she will face from you will either be general questions about her as a person and her experiences, or specific questions about her skills and experience that relate to the job for which she is applying. Also, talk to her about giving open ended explanations to the questions instead of the much less informative "yes" or "no" answers.

As she gets older and masters the Standard Interview, you will spend more time during the pre-interview Weekly Meetings explaining the intricacies of the Behavioral Interview. Once she hits about twelve years old and you think she's ready for a greater challenge, surprise her with a Behavioral Interview. After you make the phone call inviting her to interview, send her a follow-up letter in the mail. In the letter you will explain the parameters of the interview. For example, you could have a paragraph saying:

"Congratulations on obtaining an interview for such and such position. Your interview is scheduled for such and such date and time and will be a Behavioral Interview. You will have 45 minutes to answer 8 questions. You will not be cut off during any of your answers, but any questions you don't get to in the 45 minute time limit will count against you. Thank you and best of luck."

As you can see this interview technique amps up the stress from the beginning. Do some research and determine exactly how you want to conduct your interview and then have fun with it. When you administer the Behavioral Interview you will start it by reading from a script that you will write, which will be similar to the letter you sent her and then you'll dive right into the interview.

The first Weekly Meeting you have after your daughter submits a resume for a new job will always cover or be a refresher of the types of interviews, the questions and processes for each interview type and anything else you feel is relevant. When you get your daughter to the Behavioral Interview section, don't forget to teach her the categories of questions, how to study for the interview and the three-step process to answering the questions.

Weekly Meeting 2—How to Dress for Success—

As stated earlier, the interview is a formal process and this second Weekly Meeting, after the resume is submitted, is the time that you will cover such questions as how to dress, proper demeanor, how to act and what to bring with you to the interview. I once heard the phrase, "Dress for the job you want, not the job you have." Proper dress for a job interview is business attire regardless of the position for which your daughter is applying. A good lesson to teach is that she can never be overdressed for a job interview. If she is applying to flip hamburgers in full business attire, then great! That portrays the message that she is responsible and has greater aspirations than just flipping burgers, and no employer ever turns down an applicant for acting too professional. Sending this type of message is important, because if your daughter sends the message that she is motivated, then her interviewer will assume that she is a hard worker. Wearing a suit gives the impression that she takes herself and the position that she is applying for seriously and that she is sharp, organized and pays attention to details, which are all good qualities in an employee. A question I hear a lot is, "If the business is a casual environment and I know the interviewer will be in a polo shirt, doesn't it show that I understand the company well if I show up dressed just like the interviewer?" Again . . . No. Teach your kids to pay the utmost respect to people who are in a position of authority in the company in which they are trying to get hired. Period. The bottom line is that all interviews are done in a suit, regardless of the position and regardless of gender.

Business Attire—

For the boys: black, grey or navy blue suit, white shirt, subdued tie (multiple tones of one color is okay, multiple colors is not), round tipped shoes (no squared toes), no jewelry, and no cologne. For the girls: black, grey or navy blue suit, pants are preferred, but a skirt that falls just below the knee is okay, conservative white blouse, low or no heel (no open toe shoes), stud earrings only and not more than one per earlobe, and no perfume. Fragrances and jewelry are highly personal items and some people get extremely put off by certain styles or fragrances. No one is ever offended by someone looking and smelling clean. Expressing too much individuality portrays that your daughter is an individual and that she doesn't play by other people's rules; employers don't want to see that. Even if it's true, she'll have to wait until her first day on the job to express her individuality, but she can't bring it to the interview. A job interview is not the right time to buck the system or assert individuality; conformity is the key. This second pre-interview Weekly Meeting is where you teach your child how to dress, and try not to laugh when you see him standing there, at nine years old, in a full business suit.

Have you ever applied for a position where there were a number of applicants being interviewed in succession? One where each of you had to sit in a lobby and stare uncomfortably at each other, while you each got called in one at a time? I once interviewed for a position where the letter I received inviting me to the interview stated specifically to wear business attire. As we sat there, I sized up my competition and I knew that I would get the position before I even entered the interview. One gentleman was wearing tan pants with a blue shirt and brown jacket; now I'm not saying he didn't look nice, but he didn't know how to dress professionally. I also saw a lot of plastic shoes instead of leather, multicolored striped ties and ties that were not tied correctly. The knot on the tie should fill half the space between the bottom tips of the collar, so if you're trying to figure out whether a single or a double knot is correct, then look at the width of the collar tips. A narrow collar with a double knot looks pompous, and a wide collar with a single knot looks weak. The lesson you want your son or daughter to walk away with here is that the real key to looking professional has to do with putting the correct clothes on correctly, not with buying expensive or name brand clothing.

Teach your children what business attire is and how to wear it correctly. If you're not sure about the details yourself, then pick up a book on the topic; there are millions of them.

Weekly Meeting 3—Shopping

The likelihood of your nine-year-old having a suit is probably not too good, so during your third pre-interview Weekly Meeting you will have to take your son or daughter to buy some business attire. She will have to pay for it herself, of course, so hopefully she's not flat broke by this point. If Miss Reckless is broke by this time, and remember you can't extend her credit yet because she doesn't have a job, then she will have to make the money to buy her clothes. She can get some early birthday money, wash the car, or anything you can come up with to get the money to buy the necessary business attire for her big upcoming interview, but do whatever it takes. If her monetary constraints force you to take her to a second-hand store, then so be it. Some of the nicest name brand clothes I own are from a second-hand store.

Weekly Meeting 4—Dress Rehearsal

Once your daughter knows what type of interview she will face, has studied her answers to potential questions, and you've gone out and obtained the requisite articles of clothing and taught her how to wear them, it's time for a dress rehearsal. Get her all dressed up and let her get used to how her suit looks and feels. Your final pre-interview Weekly Meeting should include an interview rehearsal. Let her practice answering a few questions in front of you, but don't give away the farm, here. The rehearsal should be a mock interview aimed at bringing to light the questions she needs to think harder about before she walks into the interview.

Nervous Habits (Demeanor)—

Intuitively you might think this section should be discussed during week two, when you discuss demeanor and sitting up straight in her chair, but since your daughter's nervous habits are not likely to come to light until the dress rehearsal, we are going to cover it here, in week four.

The next important aspect of interview preparation is acting the part of a professional. Everyone has nervous habits that need to be controlled. Each person's nervous habits are different: from biting or picking at fingernails, twirling hair, tapping a pencil, rocking or swinging in the chair, to talking too fast or stumbling over words, it's your job to identify your daughter's idiosyncrasies and help her to overcome them during times of stress. These nervous habits are a way for the body to relieve stress, but to an onlooker they make us look insecure, afraid, and show a general lack of self-confidence.

An important note here is that it is your job as a Mentor to identify these traits and try to build in your daughter enough self-confidence (through repetition) that these traits disappear on their own in the interview setting. Anyone who has tried to completely stop any one of these bad habits knows it simply can't be done. We will always revert back to them when we don't feel in control. Telling your daughter to stop one of these behaviors will not work, and it will just make her feel bad about herself. Instead, give her enough practice preparing for and going through interviews that interviewing becomes old hat, and thus ceases to cause her stress. By getting rid of the stress instead of attacking her bad habit, you will get the result you want; a calm, cool, well-dressed professional sitting in front of you during these interviews.

Respect—

Respect. Regardless of what the rules are around the house, whether stifling or Woodstockesque, the rules for interaction with The Family Bank are simple; they are always formal. Your daughter will always address you as Sir or Ma'am, or Mr. or Ms. (your last name). When you are her Mentor she will call you Mom or Dad, but when dealing with The Family Bank, it's please, thank you, yes Sir and no Ma'am. One last point here is to teach your daughter to remember the names of her interviewers and to use them whenever she addresses them during the interview. It's important to end every interview with: "Thank you, Ms. (Last Name), for taking the time to interview me today. I hope to hear back from you very soon."

As you can see, there is a lot to cover between getting the interview and having the interview, which is why I recommend having at least three Weekly Meetings, if not four, before the big day. If this is your daughter's first interview, then you will want to give it four Weekly Meetings, so you will have enough time to explain the interview and hiring process, the different types of interviews, go shopping for clothes and to have a dress rehearsal before the big day.

In summary, explain to your nine-year-old that everything in the world costs money and that no one gives away money for free. People earn money by trading their valuable time for a paycheck and we call this "a job". In order to get a job we have to be qualified for the job and we have to be able to present ourselves and our qualifications in the best possible light to the people who are looking to hire us, and we only have a very limited amount of time to do it. Presenting the best possible image of ourselves consists of dressing for the part, controlling our nervous habits, treating everyone with dignity and respect and being thoroughly prepared for the interview. With everything up to this point being said and done . . . it's time for the big day.

Chapter 12

The Interview

The actual interview needs to be harder than your son expected going into it. By now, you have probably created a mental image of what the interview will be like and how you want to run it. That's perfect; just keep a couple things in mind. First, the interview always needs to be harder than your son expected it would be, and second, you are not going to hire every applicant who puts in an application to The Family Bank.

Many people believe that absolutely any failure will smash your son's self-confidence forever. Although you don't want to continuously put down or point out every flaw in your son or daughter, sometimes they have to fail. What was that? Did you read that right? Yes, sometimes they have to fail. Your son will not be qualified for every job to which he applies, but even if he is, he's not always going to give you his best performance.

To Hire or Not to Hire—

If you trap yourself into the idea that you will never "reject" your son, then you are setting both of you up to fail. Like any fourteen-year-old, he will eventually get to that point where he treats everything like a joke or at least stops taking everything you say completely seriously. You'll notice the first time he comes into an interview with that certain egotistical air about him. When you get an answer to your question like, "You already know the answer to that question" or "I don't know, whatever", or any answer to one of your questions that isn't a typical, respectful response, you will terminate the interview and say, "Thank you very much for your interest in this position, we'll get back to you as soon as we make a decision."

The general rule is that you are going to hire him as long as he puts forth his best effort and is qualified for the position. If he makes some glaring mistake in the interview, like telling you that his greatest weakness is that he's unreliable (if it's the truth), then you should still hire him. You will of course be taking notes during the interview to remind yourself of his answers later on down the road, and if some of his answers were not good interview answers then you will need to work on those answers during your next Weekly Meeting sessions. You will have to find a balance between being too harsh and being too soft, so keep this in mind: an "A" for effort means hired, where an "F" for effort or disrespect means not hired.

You will reserve the "not hired" stamp for willful displays of disrespect or being unprepared. The other circumstance where you will be forced to not hire him is if he applies to a position for which he is not qualified. After your son has been successful in Entry Level positions for about a year you will begin posting Associate level positions to which you believe your son is qualified. However, you also want to throw some Low-Level Management, Mid-Level Management and Executive positions up on that cork board, too. We are all motivated to do better and work harder when we are working toward a goal. Your ten-year-old might only be qualified for an Associate level position paying $20 per week, but seeing an Executive position on the board that pays $150 per week will look extremely enticing. By posting these positions you give your son a realistic view of the working world, where there are always better jobs just sitting there waiting to be had.

You Must Be Prepared—

Hand in hand with preparing your son for his big interview is making sure that you are also prepared. The key to success is to give yourself 10 minutes at some point during the week to look up or make up interview questions. After you've been doing this for a couple of years you will have a huge bank of questions saved to choose from, but in the beginning you need to make sure you don't go into the interview empty handed and flounder trying to think of questions to ask during the interview.

Dress appropriately. You don't have to wear a suit and tie unless the position to which your son is applying would require it. If he wants to mow the lawn, then you are a landscaping company CEO and a polo shirt with slacks will suffice. If the position is cleaning the house, then as the CEO you would probably own that company (not clean houses) and, therefore, be in a suit. Just remember that you lead by example, so regardless of the position to which your child is applying, you should be as dressed up as is logically reasonable.

I mentioned before that the interview has to be harder and more stressful than your son was anticipating. You will achieve this by maintaining rigid formality and by being thoroughly prepared for the interview, yourself. But that's not all; you will also save a surprise question for every interview. For each interview you are going to come up with a surprise question (Google them) that really challenges your son to think on his feet and articulate a thoughtful response on the spot. For example, "What do you know about our company?" or "Explain why you get the grades that you do" or "Describe your ideal job." Although the idea of a surprise question might seem new to you, every interview I have ever had has seemed to involve questions for which I was inevitably not prepared. Most employers don't purposefully hit applicants with obscure questions, but realistically it is not possible to anticipate every question an employer will ask during an interview. Most people fall apart under the combined pressure of a stressful interview *and* an unanticipated question, and thus blurt out a lackluster answer just to relieve that stress. Unfortunately, there are few opportunities to shine during an interview and any lame answers will hide your son in the group, not help him stand out from it. Your son has to be trained to cope with stress and to have the ability to generate articulate answers under pressure. This is why you will throw in a surprise question into each interview.

If your son is well prepared, then your surprise question should be the only one he stumbles on, and the next time he applies for a job he will immediately begin to dread the "surprise question" that he knows is coming. Working through some difficulty with the surprise question is no excuse for not having thoughtful answers to basic questions, though, like "Why do you think you will be successful in this job?" Expect high quality answers for the basic questions and expect some difficulty with the surprise question. In the end you want your son to be able to walk into any interview with confidence and be able to field any question on the spot, no matter how obscure, without getting flustered. As long as your son is well prepared, he'll always land his Family Bank job.

As we discussed, the interview itself must be formal, so it'll be your responsibility to set the stage. You'll conduct your interviews at The (Your Last Name) Family Bank, so make sure you have an uncomfortable chair for your son and something nicer for yourself. Make sure your desk is clean and orderly, and that the general environment is as Spartan as you can get it. Starting with Low-Level Management positions, if you have other family members who can sit in "on the board" with you, then that's great. Every board member must be dressed up in business attire. If your interview is scheduled for 4pm, then make sure your son is ready and sitting in your "waiting room" (any room you want that's not your Family Bank) by ten minutes prior. When it's time for the interview, walk to where he is sitting, give him a firm handshake, introduce yourself and walk him into the interview room. If you have board members, then introduce your son to each of the board members by their respective name and title. Once everyone is settled, ask "Do you have any questions for me before we get started?" Then launch into the interview. When it's all over thank your son for coming in and let him know you'll re-contact him within the next week.

Chapter 13

The Callback

The "dreaded callback", that is. In the real world your daughter won't always get a callback, but with The Family Bank she will. The logistics of the call back are simple; call her on the phone two days after her interview, ask for Miss (her last name) and give her one of two responses. If the interview went well, then tell her you were very impressed with her resume and interview and would like to extend her an offer of employment. If this is in the first few years, then the offer of employment will be during the phone call and you will simply schedule her first day of work. If this job position is in the later years, then you will confirm her email address and tell her that the Offer of Employment will be emailed to her shortly. In the email version of the official Offer of Employment you want to include all the basic information of the position that was listed in the original job posting and also include a start date, time and location. Of course, if you don't have a home computer you can hand write or type the Offer of Employment and send it to her via snail mail.

The other type of callback is the one that's *not* fun. In fact, don't be surprised if you get incredibly nervous the first time you have to call your son and give him the rejection notice over the phone. Even though a rejection is difficult, if it has to be done, then it has to be done, and it has to be done over the phone and by you. Remember, you will never arbitrarily reject your son after a good interview. The only time you will reject him is if he applied for a position for which he legitimately was not qualified, he had a bad attitude in (or about) the interview or he didn't prepare for it and really bombed the whole interview. If you have to give a rejection, then make the phone call two days after the interview and inform him that he was not selected for the position and inform him of the reasons why he was not selected. Also let him know that he can reapply for the position in the future if his circumstances change and he becomes better qualified for the job.

The call back is a mildly stressful time for both you and him, but it will become easier as you become more proficient with The Family Bank Financial System. It's the moment of truth, when all the preparation, or lack thereof, comes to light. Once the call back is complete and the Offer of Employment is officially extended and accepted, the next stage is sending the little man to work.

SECTION IV

Professional Development

The key element to keep in mind when it comes to Family Bank employment is to emulate the form and function of reality as best you can. This means to utilize the same basic principles with your daughter's employment that you follow at your own job, such as: work days and weekends, vacation time, sick days, write-ups, awards, bonuses and the dreaded pink slip if it has to come to that. I can't give you an *exact* outline to follow here, because every job will be different, but I'll cover the general principles for successful Family Bank Financial System employment.

Chapter 14

Rules of the Daily Grind

Most of us have a five day work week and work about forty hours, if we work full time; however, a forty hour work week for your daughter would probably fall somewhere in the realm of child labor law infraction! We definitely want to emulate the level of commitment that comes with having a full-time job, so try to keep the work week at five days with two days off; however, we'll cut a little off the actual work day to keep everything reasonable. Kids don't have much time and experience under their belts, so to them even a one month commitment can seem like an eternity.

When I was in elementary school, every school year seemed like a lifetime. I'd have sworn that Christmases were ten years apart, but now the years fly! This sense of time is a tool you can use to teach your children long-term commitment for things like college and a career. An important quality to instill in children at a young age is the ability persist in a long-term commitment, and luckily The Family Bank is the perfect tool for just such a lesson. I have a lot of friends who didn't make it through college because "it wasn't their thing", but the real problem was that no one ever helped them develop the ability to see that type of long-term commitment through to the end. Using a five day work week over an extended period of time teaches your children the ability to see employment, and even school, as a long-term, achievable routine.

The question, and ultimately the lesson here, is how to teach your daughter to persist in a long-term commitment, given the fact that she has an underdeveloped attention span. Little Miss "I'm bored" will quickly tire of working. In the beginning your daughter's work day will have to be very short, so it will be up to you to finagle the length of the "duty day" that works best for your child. Your daughter's first job has to require a very short work day or you will find that you don't have the energy to "remind" her every day to do it. For example, gathering up all the garbage in the house and taking it out to the trash can is a great first job. Taking out the garbage is a short task that can be finished in about five to ten minutes per day. What's important here is not to do a lot of work everyday, but to establish the routine of setting aside the time to go to work five days per week, every week. Your daughter learning to work hard, and to take satisfaction from a job well done, will come a little later, after you have established the framework for how employment actually works.

When she gets a little older and is functioning well in her established work routine, the new jobs you post will require a somewhay longer work day, as we discussed earlier in the Searching for Employment chapter. The goal is to stretch her attention span, but not to break it. All the work she does has to be quality work, so if she is working for too long each day for her age level, after a while she will start to dilly-dally and complain about having to go to work.

Once your daughter reaches fifteen years old, you will create all sorts of Executive job positions and it will be up to her how much she wants to work and how much money she wants to make. The only rules I really try to stick to when it comes to work days is that she works five days per week and not for longer each day than her attention span can handle. Also, the work days don't have to be Monday through Friday. If her job is a basic "cleaning the house" type position, then I suggest making her work days Thursday through Monday, so the house gets cleaned right before, during, and then again right after the weekend.

Also, don't make work days that fall on Saturday or Sunday longer than during the week workdays. That is not how real employment works, so don't teach lessons that don't translate to the real world just for the sake of convenience. Every job listing you create should have a consistent amount of work that needs to be accomplished each day. Also, if she has to call in sick for a couple of days, you can't hold that against her and make her "make up" the work. If her job is to take out the trash after dinner every night, and she calls in sick for two days in a row, then you have to take out the trash in her place. Just like real employment, the world goes on without us when we call in sick.

The length of the duty day will end up pretty structured until around age fifteen, which is when she will also start to get interested in real employment and making "big money". At this point, you will have to discuss her employment goals with her and coordinate her Family Bank Financial System employment with real world employment. Ideally, you are going to want to introduce her to the idea of starting her own business about this age, which will also open up a slew of opportunities for both of you, but we will talk more about starting her own business a little later. Suffice it to say that age fifteen is where the hard and fast rules of The Family Bank Employment end, and your own creativity coupled with your daughter's financial desires take over.

When your daughter gets to the age that she starts considering outside employment, there are certain factors you will have to take into consideration, like whether or not you want her to work outside your home. If you don't want her to obtain outside employment quite yet, just emphasize that if she gets an outside job, she will have to continue to use every other aspect of The Family Bank. This means she will still have to pay you for her rent and bills. If you're not supplying her paycheck, but you're still collecting $400 per month in rent, she might not be so inclined to leave. On the other hand, you may want your daughter to get a real job, in which case you can renegotiate her rent and other expenses down to a minimal amount, say $100 per month. You'll never completely get rid of her expenses, as those are part of teaching her how to budget and how to handle money, but you are ultimately in control of The Family Bank and you must utilize it how you see fit.

If you don't want your kids to work outside the home before age eighteen, your job postings will have to be for Executive level positions requiring more hours of work per day and paying a salary commensurate to real employment, let's say $150 per week. If $150 a week still seems like too much money, just consider how much it would cost you to buy all her clothes, school supplies and give her money to go out on the weekends if she wasn't working outside the home! At least with employment in The Family Financial System you get some work done around the house for the money you give her. I use $150 dollars as an arbitrary number here, as some people can only afford $10 dollars per week and others may be able to spare a thousand. The point here is that you have an element of control over what your kids do for work outside the home and your sole influence does not consist of the phrase "because I said so!"

Having grown up all her life working for The Family Bank, your daughter is going to be comfortable doing so, as long as she can make enough money to get by. If she wants to try her hand at real employment, though, I encourage you to encourage her. In the end, the whole reason for creating The Family Bank is to teach your children how to be successful in the real world and what better way is there to test those skills than to let her find a real job?

Lastly, some rules for Family Bank Employment. She will always have a start time and an end time, and either a uniform or dress code for work. It is important that she establishes a routine for getting ready and showing up for work on time from the very beginning. So, if her first job is taking out the garbage Thursday through Monday at 8pm, then she needs to be standing in front of you before every shift in the correct outfit by no later than 7:55pm. Keep in mind that if you want her to wear a uniform, like a polo shirt and khaki pants, then you have to provide her with your company uniform, just like any other employer would do. When she gets a little older and lands her first Executive position, then she should be showing up for work in either the proper attire, or a business suit that she bought herself, just like we discussed in the interview preparation section. If your daughter is the Head Chef of your household, then you should just give her requirements for how she dresses during work hours and then provide her with a nice chef's hat! Employment in The Family Bank is not simply a list of chores to do each day, it's a small scale model of real world employment for the purpose of preparing her for how the real world works. Therefore, above all else, try to always maintain realism, which starts with a five day work week, but can end up as complicated and interesting as you'd like to make it.

Chapter 15

Vacation and Sick Time

Vacations and sick time are a vital aspect of Family Bank Employment. Whenever we start something new—a new project at home, a new diet, a new exercise plan, etc.—let's just say that it often gets abandoned about a month after we start. So knowing that our children can't abandon The Family Bank Employment for any reason, we need a system in place to keep them on track. I'm not reinventing the wheel, here. How is it that you are able to continue working at your job for twenty years, but that New Year's resolution only lasted a month? Yes, scheduled and unscheduled time-off, with a non-negotiable time to return to work, otherwise known as vacation time and sick days.

Your Entry and Associate level positions should start off accruing vacation at a rate of two days per month (not 24 days per year), then three days per month for Low-level and Mid-level management and four days per month for Executive positions. Remember, time moves along on a different scale for children than it does for adults, so you'll always want to shorten up time measurements in The Family Bank: years to months, months to weeks and weeks to days. You'll also want to allow vacation time to be submitted on fairly short notice. Kids' schedules are often busy and change quickly, so 24-hour notice should be standard for vacation time.

Encourage your daughter to take vacation time when she needs time off for activities that conflict with work and to coordinate with family vacations. Also, teach her to plan in advance. If she knows that a family vacation is coming up, then she needs to make sure she accrues enough vacation time to cover the family vacation. Of course, you can't fire her if the family vacation sneaks up and she doesn't have enough time accrued to cover it, or worse yet you decide to take a last minute family vacation and she wasn't given enough notice to save up the vacation time, so here is where you introduce her to "leave without pay". If she failed to save up enough vacation time when she had enough notice, then the loss of pay for that time period makes for a pretty good self-inflicted punishment. If she didn't have enough notice from you that vacation was coming up, then it's a good lesson on maintaining a bank of vacation time for last second emergencies; it's a win-win situation for you.

It's also important to teach the distinction between vacation time and sick time very early. Vacation is for desired time off *and* emergencies, sick days are for when she's sick. Let sick days accrue at one day per month across the different levels of employment. Sick days won't increase in number as the level of employment increases; just because you're an executive doesn't mean you get sick more often. In the real world, higher level employment may come with more sick days, of course, but that doesn't help you teach the right lesson about not using "sick days" as "personal days". If it seems like some sections of The Family

Bank are as close to reality as possible and other sections differ from how the real world works, then you're on to something. As a general rule, we want to teach our kids how the real world works. However, more importantly, we are teaching our kids how to be successful in the real world. Some aspects of real world employment cause problems for adults. These problem areas are where we deviate a little from real world procedures in order to teach very specific lessons geared at steering our kids away from making these common mistakes.

So let's get back to sick days and how they work. In the real world the higher the level of the position you obtain in a company the more sick days you get. However, young people, new to the employment realm, often get in trouble using sick days like personal days when they are not really sick. If your job postings were to include an increase in sick days, that would be confusing; if sick days increased like vacation time, it would seem logical that your children could use them like vacation time, even if they're not really sick. In your daughter's mind, having a better job doesn't mean you get sick more often, so sick days shouldn't increase unless you're supposed to use them all, right? In order to help them make the connection that you can only use sick days when you are actually sick, the number of sick days shouldn't increase with higher level position job postings. Teach your daughter to call in sick only when she is actually sick and to plan ahead and take vacation time for any other time that she needs off. Also, the rate of accrual of vacation time is just a guideline, not set in stone. If your family requires your daughter to have a little more or a little less vacation time, then alter it how you see fit.

Ideally, your daughter will only try to use sick days when she is actually sick, and as long as that is the case you shouldn't question her about it. Don't pretend to be a suspicious boss. Teach her that it's okay to call in sick if she really is sick. If she tries to call in sick when she isn't really sick, though, then you are going to have to call her out on it. Let her know that when she comes back to work she will have to have a doctor's note. Of course, in order to get a doctor's note she will have to get Mom or Dad to write it, which they won't do if she isn't really sick. So, once she gets "called out" on calling in sick when she isn't really sick . . . where do you go from there? Funny you should ask.

Chapter 16

Write-ups

Getting written up, although unpleasant, is a part of any and every job and so it is part of Family Bank employment. The Family Bank utilizes the same system for correcting undesirable behavior that most employers use: Verbal Warning, Written Warning, Letter of Reprimand, and finally, Termination.

Verbal Warning—

The first step in the process, and arguably the least effective, (especially for children, as I believe they are born immune to this) is the Verbal Warning. The first time Mr. Sleepyhead shows up late for work, calls in sick when he isn't really sick, doesn't do a good job at work or for any reason that connotes less than satisfactory job performance, you will have a nice "sit down" and give him his first Verbal Warning. Take him to the desk at The Family Bank and let him know that an issue has been brought to your attention and that that kind of behavior is not conducive to his continued employment.

This is when you will explain to him the disciplinary system. Tell him that when his job performance does not meet a satisfactory level put forth by this company, then certain predetermined steps will have to be taken. This is the first step, which is his Verbal Warning. The next step is a Written Warning, documenting the continuing issue, which will be placed in his file at work. The third step in the process is a Letter of Reprimand that will come with some form of disciplinary action, which could include but is not limited to a reduction of pay, either temporary or permanent, or a temporary suspension. The final step in the disciplinary process is Termination. Then send him on his merry way back to work.

Written Warning—

The second step in the process will come after a second violation of either a similar incident or a second incident that speaks to a particular recurring problem. If your son shows up late to work one day and you give him a Verbal Warning, and the next day he leaves his shift fifteen minutes early without asking you first, then the problem is responsibility and reliability, and you will proceed to the second step in the disciplinary process. If he is late to work one day and the next day he does a bad job cleaning the bathroom, then a second Verbal Warning is in order, for poor work performance.

You will type up a Written Warning on your company letterhead with his name and employment information, which will explain the reason for the Written Warning and what is expected of him in the future to avoid further disciplinary action. For example, you will write something like:

"On Saturday, May 14th, 2012, you showed up for work at 4:15pm when your shift was scheduled from 4pm to 4:30pm. On Sunday, May 15th, 2012, you left work at 4:15pm when your shift was scheduled from 4pm to 4:30 pm. Not working the correct hours according to your scheduled work times shows a pattern of being unreliable and irresponsible. From this day forward you are expected to be at work and ready to work at the beginning of your scheduled shift and you will be expected to work the entire duration of your scheduled shift. Failure to comply with this written notice will result in further disciplinary action."

Letter of Reprimand—

Hopefully, you'll never get to this step; but just in case you do, I should also cover the Letter of Reprimand. Now these can be done many different ways, but I find that the simplest way is usually the best way (which is a good rule when it comes to almost anything). The severity of the Letter of Reprimand should depend on one thing; whether your son got into this situation willfully or through carelessness. If your son is slow on his feet and shows up five minutes late for work on a regular basis, then the big teaching point here is time management. If the reason for the letter is shoddy work ethic or leaving work ten minutes early every day to go play with friends, then the issue at hand is acting willfully disobedient. So the two major issues that come into play with the Letter of Reprimand are the severity of the punishment and the issue that is causing the necessity of the letter in the first place. Both of these issues will have to be dealt with, both in the Letter of Reprimand and your next Weekly Meeting.

The severity of the punishment incurred by the Letter of Reprimand will depend on the level of the position your son is in, his age and maturity level, and other factors only you will be able to determine, such as his current financial situation or if he is saving vacation time for a particular trip. The Letter of Reprimand is also written on your company letterhead and should say "Letter of Reprimand" written across the top of the page in red ink. Although an actual Letter of Reprimand is not usually written like this, you will be giving this letter to your child and it needs to drive home your point. The letter should read something like:

> *"You,* (child's name) *are receiving this official Letter of Reprimand due to continued failure to* (specify the reason for the letter). *Due to your continuing actions you are being placed on Administrative Leave without Pay for* (you choose how long). *During this time you will not be allowed to work and your pay will be suspended along with benefits such as accrual of vacation time. You will not be permitted to take accrued vacation time to supplement your pay during this period of time. After* (however long you decided) *you will return to work with full reinstatement of pay and benefits, but will remain on general probation for a period of* (you choose how long). *Any new or continued violations of company policy during this probation will result in the immediate termination of your employment with* (the name of your company, i.e. Family Lawn Care Service or Family Housekeeping Service). *After your general probation period you will remain on specific, indefinite probation for* (whatever the reason was for the Letter of Reprimand, i.e. showing up late for work)."

Remember that willful disobedience should be punished more severely than issues arising from negligence, but just because your son "accidentally" sleeps through his alarm for the third time doesn't mean he is going to get off easy.

The Weekly Meeting that you have with your son after he receives his official Letter of Reprimand needs to focus on resolving the issue that led up to receiving the letter in the first place. So, if Mr. Sleepyhead is regularly showing up late to work, then it's time to have the "ten minutes early is on time, on time is late and late is fired" talk. Every situation is different, so relate to him, give him examples from your own life and get him on the right track. Also, keep in mind that he has already been punished by his boss at work for the issue. You need to be supportive and teach him what it means to be a responsible working adult. Don't take this time to focus on telling him how wrong he was and don't overlap your roles of "CEO" and "Mentor". When you are Mom you are always the good guy in The Family Bank. The real world is cold and unforgiving and the idea is to teach your kids how to get along in the real world, but also to teach your son that he can always come back to Mom and Dad for advice or to "vent" about how unfair his boss is being. The reason I talk about maintaining the role of the good guy / Mentor at all times while in the Weekly Meetings will become very apparent in the next chapter.

Chapter 17

Termination

Even though firing your daughter from her Family Bank Job seems like a logical progression on the disciplinary scale, I gave "Termination" its own chapter because it really is its own separate issue. Terminating your daughter's employment is, and I can't emphasize this enough, your absolute very last option. If it were feasible, I would say that you should never fire your daughter under any circumstances, but if I said that, then you might as well burn the rest of this book, because this is a guide to teaching your children how to get along and be successful in the real world, and not a how-to guide on building egos or arrogance.

Having said that, it is possible to teach your daughter about the "real world" and build her self-confidence at the same time, but for that you have to truly understand the difference between being a CEO and being a Mentor. The duality of your roles allows you to expose your daughter to the harshness of reality with one hand, while cushioning the blow with the other. I'm guessing you read that remark and either thought "don't tap dance around, kids need to learn some lessons the hard way" *or* "I'll just cut out the whole firing chapter and no one will be the wiser". Well, give me the opportunity to explain to both of you that the only correct way to teach this lesson is right down the middle . . .

Why we can't be too rough . . .

Different kids have different personalities and different abilities to handle stress before they shut down, and all your hard work is lost. If you feel you need to teach your daughter to be tough in an unforgiving world by showing her no mercy, then keep reading.

If I wanted to teach you pain tolerance, it's been documented that subjecting you to slowly increasing amounts of pain can be effective. But if I kill you in the process, then my lesson is lost no matter how good my intentions were. Some kids can handle a lot of stress before they close off and stop listening to you, but other kids close up much sooner, and closing off is not something you, as a parent, can "push her through". The fact that different kids can handle different levels of stress not only holds true for different children in the same family . . . but *especially* for different children in same family; so don't Mentor all your kids the same way. Some children will need you to help them work through the logical reasons why they got fired, whereas some children will need more emotional support.

You don't need to be an expert in child psychology in order to use The Family Bank; all you need to do is maintain a balance between being the CEO and being the Mentor. Use the CEO to teach the cold, hard lessons, but don't also use the Mentor to try to reteach a lesson that has already been taught by the CEO. If your employer hired another person to walk behind you and redo everything you do at work, that would really upset you. So don't redo all your own work! When you are Mom or Dad the Mentor, take that time for what it is, the time for you to be the person your child can turn to when things are going badly for her. Teach her how to problem solve and how to not make the same mistakes again, but don't beat a dead horse telling her over and over why she got fired. Weekly Meetings are the time that you will Mentor your child, listen to what she has to say and teach her the ways of the world. Eventually, your daughter will move away from home and the CEO will retire, but the Mentor is a position held for life, so make it a cherished position.

The Weekly Meeting after Miss Unemployed gets fired needs to focus on how to apply for a new job, how to rewrite her resume, and how to write a letter of apology to her previous employer in an attempt not to leave that position with such a bad reference. Mentoring should focus on the future and not dwell in the past. The bottom line is not to soften the blow of getting fired, but rather to give her the skills and abilities to move forward. Every so often you should be taking your daughter out for ice cream for your Weekly Meeting and discussing how things are going for her financially, at her job, in school, etc. and after getting fired is not the time to stop those outings. If you take her out for ice cream as her Mentor after she gets fired, don't consider that to be a reward for getting fired; it's not. If she needs time to relax with you and talk about things, then do that! It doesn't change the fact that she just lost her job, and don't forget how you would feel if you just lost your job. Making your daughter feel bad about failing does not make her tough, it makes her resentful. When she needs a mentor, be a Mentor.

Why not to be too gentle . . .

I think the general idea is clear, but I have to put my two cents in here, too. If you excel at being the Mentor and find you have difficulty doing your duty as the CEO, then I can't let you off easy, either. The world really is cold and unforgiving, and no matter how much self-confidence and self-esteem your son has, if he has never felt rejection or denial from The Family Bank, then he won't know how to cope with it when he turns eighteen years old. We covered the duality of the CEO and the Mentor, but the most important point to remember is that they are equal roles. As the CEO you have to be tough, cold and always do what is in the best interest of your company, not one individual worker; that's reality.

Your son has to learn that there is an accepted way to operate in a work environment. Be on time, be respectful of his superiors, take initiative at work and don't treat work like a game. If you make the decision that you will never fire him, regardless of the circumstances, before you even start your Family Bank, then you have already failed him. He will go out into the world feeling that he is more important than the company he works for, and as true as that is, he won't go far in his career once his employer sees that attitude. If your son is coming in late to work every day because he doesn't think you will do anything about it, and somehow you manage to muster up the nerve to give him a one day suspension, after which he comes in late again the next day . . . now what? If you're not willing to embrace the role of CEO and terminate him, then you've trapped yourself.

The Family Bank is meant to teach your kids how the real world works and how to be amazingly successful functioning within it. So here is what you will do . . . see below. The Family Bank CEO will fire him and The Family Bank Mentor will counsel him. Not fulfilling your role as the CEO is equally damaging as not fulfilling your role as Mentor. The moral of the story is to put your full effort into both jobs, and to push yourself a little in the area you know is naturally more difficult for you.

Firing your child is a big and painful responsibility that you possess as the CEO of The Family Bank and utilizing it is vitally important to your child's future success. Take that middle road where you do both your duty as the CEO, and fulfill your obligation as the Mentor. Having said all of this, the question is: "how do you actually fire her?"

How to Terminate—

If you thoroughly explained the disciplinary process before all this began, then she should already know what's coming. So, the only thing left is to give her the termination letter. Again, like the Written Notice and the Letter of Reprimand, the Termination Notice will be written on your company letterhead. You will write:

> *"Due to continued violations of company policy* (then outline the violations)*"* or *"Due to a continued lack of discipline and reliability* (again, explain) *your position at The Family Housecleaning Service* (or whatever your company name is) *has been terminated effective immediately. Your final paycheck will be mailed to you for the hours you worked during this pay period."*

It should be short, simple and to the point.

Your daughter may take her termination very hard, in which case the Mentor will need to step up his game, but more likely she'll act as though she doesn't care. The older your daughter is at the time she receives her Termination Notice, the less likely she is to care about it, at first. Don't get discouraged. The lesson will get through. She will see the ramifications of getting fired when she stops receiving a paycheck. Then, when her money runs out and she tries to apply for a new job, she will see how difficult it is to get a new job when she can't use the old job as a reference. She will either have to leave that time period empty on her resume and then try to explain it away in an interview, or put it on the resume and deal with the consequences of a poor referral. Either way, she won't get the next job to which she applies regardless of how well she does in the interview. Not necessarily realistic? It doesn't matter. She is learning that there are serious negative consequences for getting fired and that the only way to have a successful career is to play by the rules at work.

The best punishment you can give your son for getting fired is to make your next job postings extra enticing! A low level position that requires little work and pays well, although not outrageously well, as he should see this as a legitimate opportunity and not an obvious punishment for getting fired. Nothing stings quite so much as a genuinely missed opportunity, so take advantage of your position and the power you wield with The Family Bank, to teach a valuable lesson. Remember to always be fair, but always be teaching, too.

Chapter 18

Bonuses and Raises

So what's with all the negativity? It sounds like all we focus on is discipline, but your son is an angel, and a diligent and hard worker, right? Well, that's great; we have something for everyone in The Family Bank! Although there are many schools of thought on discipline when it comes to parenting, such as: positive reinforcement (getting something good for doing something good), negative reinforcement (taking away something bad for doing something good), and punishment (we all know what that is), there is only one system when it comes to the work force. You get rewarded (never enough or fast enough) for doing well, and you get punished for doing poorly. We've covered punishment, so I guess that leaves us in the reward section.

As I mentioned earlier, rewards are never adequate or timely. Keep raises small but noticeable, about five percent of his original salary. If your son was making $10 dollars a week and he has been doing very well at work for two months, then schedule an appointment with him at work (on his work time) and give him a positive evaluation and a five percent raise. Now his killer ten dollar salary is all the way up to

$10.50 per week, and if he keeps it up he may see $11 a week sometime this year! I'm being a little facetious here, but, of course, it's for a good reason. Raises will always remain small because you want him to aspire to apply to a new job, with more responsibility and better pay. He has to move up in the world by getting better jobs or better positions within his current company. If the raises are too big then he will end up sixteen years old and making $100 a week to take out the garbage after dinner; so keep the raises small, just like your employer does!

Aside from small raises, you also want to utilize bonuses. Bonuses will only be given out if at least his last two evaluations have been perfect. Then, it's up to you to coordinate the bonuses with big upcoming events, like a family member's birthday. Don't give bonuses right before an event or it will be seen either as a gift or as something owed to him. For example, if you celebrate Christmas, then that will be a time of great financial expense to little Mr. Reckless. If his last two evaluations have been good, then you might give him a bonus of one, two, even four full weeks of pay around mid October. This teaches him that hard work and good performance are rewarded, but you are sneaking in a second lesson here, too. By giving him the money a couple of months before the holiday season, you are forcing him to plan ahead and save that money. Inevitably, the first year he will not make the association in time and he will blow all his money in October. When Black Friday rolls around and he doesn't have enough money to get all the presents on his list, he just might think (or you just might remind him), "Maybe I should have saved that $50 bonus I got last month."

Keep in mind that The Family Bank is a long-term project. Don't feel it necessary to cram every lesson into one Weekly Meeting. Some lessons can only be learned from making mistakes, as I'm sure we have all learned throughout our lives. After a mistake, though, we have to have the opportunity next time to go out and try it again the right way, in order to solidify the ideas and concepts that we learned from our previous mistakes. Concepts like saving money, borrowing money with a plan to pay it back, building credit and building a successful career are all concepts that have to be learned through trial and error, over an extended period of time. Now, if your son is seventeen and he just blew his October bonus on candy for the eighth year in a row... hmmm... at this point you may have a problem! But seriously, if your son isn't picking it all up the first time around, don't worry; he's right on track and he will get it eventually. No one gets it all right the first time. If we did there would be no need for The Family Bank in the first place.

SECTION IV

Paying Bills

Bills have to start immediately upon gaining employment, because . . . isn't that how it really works? Your daughter having to pay bills actually helps you as out in two different areas: by forcing your daughter to create of a budget, and by allowing you to pay her more money for her weekly salary. You'll be able to pay her more money because you'll know that some of that money will be coming immediately back to you in the form of her "bill payments". By dealing with bills and larger amounts of money now, your daughter will become better able to utilize and control her money later on in life.

Without bills in The Family Bank you might be able to pay your daughter $15 a week, which ends up being money out of your pocket. However, if her lunch is $40 per month, then you can pay her $25 dollars per week, because $10 per week of that money is coming right back to you! You're still only paying $15 a week out of your pocket. By dealing with paying bills, your daughter will have to create a budget. She'll feel like she is making a lot of money and, due to her bills, she will feel a responsibility to maintain her employment with The Family Bank.

Paying bills is a part of every person's everyday life, so it is only natural to add it into The Family Bank. Creating a budget that covers your son's bills and allows for him to determine the amount of extra money he has left over at the end of each month is a skill that he needs to have; yet, painfully few of us actually do. I never used to create a budget, because I felt that my finances where too complicated and inconsistent. Whenever I wrote all my bills down on paper they never seemed to match what I was actually spending. Why was that? It's all about practice. When I started driving a car in high school, it was all I could do to work the accelerator, brake pedal and clutch all at the same time, just to get the car to stop and start. Add to that the necessity of figuring out where I was supposed to be going and paying attention to the other drivers on the road at the same time . . . forget about it. Yet, now I drive every day, controlling my car and flowing in and out of traffic seamlessly, without even thinking about it. How was I able to become such a proficient driver? Well, I started early in life and I practiced, just like everyone else. So how will your son get to become proficient at creating a budget? Yup, teach him early and make it a part of his everyday life, and by the time he is fourteen years old he will be creating your family budget!

Chapter 19

Lunch Money

The first bill you are going to smack your daughter with is her lunch money. The amount you charge should reflect directly the amount you pay for her lunch. If you have an elementary 'schooler' and her hot lunch costs you $40 per month, then that is a real life bill you can pass along to your daughter; just charge her $20 per paycheck. In the beginning, you can create your own home-made bill and put it in her inbox, along with her paycheck. On bill paying day, she will write you a check for the $20 and you will deduct the check right out of her account. Down the road, you will move her into the realm of direct deposit, and after you've shown her how to set that up, you'll introduce her to automatic withdraws through her checking account or automatic payments through her credit card. And the whole world begins to come together and make sense; dollars and sense!

As your daughter gets older and becomes more and more proficient creating her budget, you can continue to stack more and more bills on her. In fact, the more the merrier! Of course, you will have to pay her more at her Family Bank job, but the more complicated you can make her monthly expenses, the more skilled she will become at creating and maintaining a budget.

Chapter 20

Rent

    Charging rent is so great on so many levels. It allows you to really boost up your son's income, so he can play around with larger sums of money and learn how to budget, but it also creates the necessity that he maintain Family Bank employment. The Family Bank and Financial System really break down, and the majority of the teaching points are lost, if your son decides he doesn't want to maintain Family Bank employment, so rent is a must. By charging rent he will always have a fairly large bill that comes due every month and without a job he will not be able to pay it. So, what happens when he decides he doesn't need a job or his room? Then he camps on the living room floor or the floor in your bedroom and the only expense you will cover for him is his food expense. He will lose complete access to his bedroom. In the end you are always his parent and you will always provide him with food and a technical "roof over his head", but he doesn't have to enjoy it! This might all sound extreme, but it works. He will loathe the loss of his privacy and you will find him applying for a Family Bank Job within days.

The second great point to renting your son his room is that there is absolutely no question about who owns it. You do. You are the landlord, so you have the right to inspect his room at any time you like. He is technically renting it from you, so you will generate a rental agreement with him that you will both sign and abide by. The best time to begin renting your son his bedroom is around age eleven or twelve. By this time, he has a good understanding of how to manage his money and generate income, so there's no time like the present to up the ante. By increasing his expenses, as we discussed earlier, it will force him to have and to hold a Family Bank job for more than just disposable income. He will have to begin learning how to budget and how to deal with larger sums of money. This is where the Weekly Meetings will take a turn towards explaining bills and adult obligations like rent and owning his own home, someday.

Have fun during this time, but also be sure to lay down the ground rules. For example, "You are eleven years old now and so the free ride is over. This is (let's say) June, so starting August 1st you must begin paying rent for your bedroom. So you should start checking the cork board for some better paying jobs and get your finances in order." Let him know that at the next Weekly Meeting you will have a rental agreement drawn up for him to look over and sign. Renting your son his bedroom is the first really big step towards turning the basics he has learned over the years into practical knowledge.

Thus far, we have covered the basics about the symbiotic relationship between banks and consumers, and how we as contributing members of society obtain and maintain employment. However, up to this point we have really just been laying the groundwork for what we are *really* trying to teach; not how to survive, but how to thrive.

SECTION V

Managing Money

This section takes a turn away from the basics that we have been discussing up to this point. You can think of the first four sections of this book as your guide to the fundamentals, while section five, six and seven bring you into the advanced course. So far, we have covered how to generate and control money, which are extremely important lessons, but those areas are not really what destroy most of us financially when we hit eighteen years old. The reason we spent so much time on the first four sections is just to make the rest of The Family Bank possible. Between the ages of 18 and 25 years old, I literally destroyed myself financially, and I know I'm not alone. I had struggled through learning most of the information covered in the first four sections through trial and error, and at the expense of a lot of real money and real missed employment opportunities. But struggling to learn section five on my own, without guidance and without a proper foundation, is what crushed me.

Section five focuses on managing money. Managing money is far more than controlling money. Controlling money means to move it around, but managing money (and credit), means that you are in charge of it, you understand it and it works for you. Yes, that's right, credit can actually be utilized, not just used. You can't delve into section five with your kids until they have mastered sections one through four and you believe that they are mature enough to move into section five. I'm not saying to wait forever, just make sure they have the basics down. The earlier your children start using anything in their lives, the more familiar with it they will become, the less scary it will become and the better they will understand it and be able to use it. The earliest you should delve into Managing Money is age ten and about the longest you should wait is age twelve. Having said that, if your daughter is fifteen years old right now, and you haven't even finished reading this book yet, then she will likely master all the fundamentals pretty quickly, so you can delve into Money Management with her after she has been using The Family Bank for a few months. Keep in mind, though, that she has to have a stable job with The Family Bank, at a bare minimum, before she can even be considered for credit.

You'll start off your next Weekly Meeting telling your daughter that you think she is now old enough to learn about credit, which, of course, is where you get the requisite, "Dad, I already know what credit cards are!" Don't laugh here and don't challenge her on that. All kids already know everything! So this will just be a reminder for her . . . a very long and complicated reminder. To all you financial gurus out there, I want you to keep one thing in mind: you are going to explain to her only the very simplest concepts of credit. If you think the following explanations are too simple and are not an exact representation of the real world, keep in mind that she is only around ten years old. The reason you are teaching her these concepts so early is so she can avoid being buried in unsecured debt when she turns eighteen years old, and for her to have a good understanding of how to use credit to her benefit when she is ready. If you are a financial advisor reading this, remember this is not a course designed to turn your ten-year-old daughter into a financial advisor. However, if your child has mastered credit by age twelve and you want to run with it and teach her everything you know, then go for it. You are her Mentor.

In this section, we are going to cover credit and interest before we cover credit cards, because that is NOT the order in which credit card companies want your kids to learn these lessons, and for good reason. By understanding interest and credit before she charges her first purchase, at least she will understand what is happening when her Family Bank debt runs out of control.

Once your daughter has built up an employment history and has mastered the art of "only spending the money she has", it's time to rattle that foundation by introducing her to the idea of spending money she does **not** have, and this of course couldn't start any other way than with a Weekly Meeting. So here it is, let's get started with credit scores, interest and forms of credit . . . or what we already know to be "the financial death trap".

Chapter 21

Credit and Your Credit Score

This first Weekly Meeting dealing with credit will be difficult, because you have to start by explaining the abstract idea of credit and a credit score. This lesson is vital, though, because the very foundation of our economy and, therefore, of The Family Bank, is credit. In order for your children to be successful in The Family Bank and later in life, they must learn how to function in a world run by credit. As you know, your daughter's credit worthiness, her very ability to function in society, is measured by her credit score. Therefore, your first credit based Weekly Meeting will start with you telling your daughter a little story that goes something like this . . .

Imagine we are at the park and you are playing with two boys whose Moms have dropped them off to play. I'm at the park with you, and before we left home I packed you a lunch with a sandwich and three cookies. At lunchtime, we sit down with the other two boys to eat lunch, but their Moms didn't pack them any cookies. Both of the other two boys are sad, and ask you if you will give them each a cookie to eat right now. They each tell you that after his Mom comes to pick him up, he will bring you back a cookie *and* he will also bring you a piece of candy, as a way to thank you for giving up one of your cookies right now. You don't want to give your cookies away, but if you give away two of your cookies right now, then each boy has promised you that later you will get your cookie back, and you will also get candy. So, you decide to give away two of your cookies, one to each of the boys.

Later that day, when their Moms come back to pick them up, one of the boys gives you back a cookie and a piece of candy just like he told you he would. The other boy goes home and doesn't give you the cookie or the candy that he promised you. The next day we all go back to the park again, and again you have three cookies at lunch. Again, the same two boys don't have any cookies, and again, they both ask you for a cookie and tell you they will give you a cookie and a piece of candy when their Moms come to pick them up. Today, though, you decide you are only going to give a cookie to the boy who paid you back yesterday, but you are not going to give your cookie to the other little boy who left yesterday and never gave you the cookie or the candy that he promised you.

Explain to your daughter that in this scenario the cookies are money and that "credit" is the idea of giving away your cookies now, if you get your cookies back later. But no one wants to give his cookies away right now just to get the same cookies back later, so to make it worthwhile to you to give up your cookies right now, people promise that they will give you back the same kind of cookies *plus* something more, like some candy, too. In our story, the candy is "interest". Credit works because people don't always have all the money they need right at the moment, so they borrow the money they need and, in return, they promise to pay it back, plus a fee (interest). The bottom line is that we are "buying" money for a price, and we pay for it later.

You can further explain, "If you want a toy that costs $10, then all you do is give the store $10 right now and they will give you the toy. But what if you don't have $10 right now? Then to get the toy right now you'll have to buy $10 from the bank. You can't give the bank $10 for the $10 they are going to give you, because if you had the $10 you wouldn't need to buy it from the bank! So, the bank agrees to give you $10 right now, if you agree to pay the the $10 dollars back to the bank later, plus "interest". So you get the $10 that you need right now to go buy that toy you want, even though you don't have any money right now, as long as you agree to pay the bank back a total of $15 next month.

The bottom line is that you can go to the bank and ask them to give you some money right now and in return you will promise to pay them back more money than they gave you. If you didn't pay them back more money than they gave you, then they would not want to give you their money right now; just like you didn't want to give away your cookies at lunch, but you did because later you ended up getting your cookies back, plus some candy.

Credit is the idea that you can borrow money from the bank right now and pay it back later; but do you remember the little boy who took your cookie the first day at the park, and when his Mom picked him up he didn't pay you back? Of course you do. Don't you wish you could have known that he wasn't going to pay you back before you gave him that first cookie? Of course you do. Well that is why people have "credit scores". Every person has a number that goes along with her credit, and every bank can see that number when she asks the bank for money. If you borrow money from a bank, but then you don't pay that money back, the bank will take points away from your "credit score" and your score will go down. The next time you try to borrow money from a bank, the new bank will look at your credit score and see that it is too low and that your first bank took points away because you didn't pay them back the money you borrowed. When the new bank sees your bad credit score they will decide to not give you any money.

Imagine you could have known, before you gave that boy the cookie, that last week he had borrowed a cookie from another little girl and never paid her back, either; imagine he had a "cookie credit score". You probably wouldn't have given him that first cookie, because he had a *bad* cookie credit score!

Make Her Credit Tangible—

Now back to the Family Bank. Our analogy is simple, but even so, depending on the age of your daughter when you introduce her to credit, you will have to explain it a couple of times. Now that she has a cursory understanding of credit, interest and her credit score, let's turn this into something tangible.

Her credit score is going to be posted on The Family Bank white board, so that it is always visible and never forgotten. The only way to turn a concept in to reality is to make it visually accessible. Of course, you will also keep her credit score calculated in your journal. Remember you will keep a journal of her bank records, and a separate journal for her credit transactions. The method you use to control and change her credit score will follow a set formula; *however*, this formula will not exactly reflect reality. In reality, computing a credit score is complicated and many factors go in to calculating it. In The Family Bank, though, we try to keep it simple so you can calculate her credit quickly and easily and she will understand it clearly. Like other sections of The Family Bank, we want to make a strong visual point and we want her credit score to change proportionately with how a ten—to twelve-year-old views the world . . . let's just say, a bit exaggerated.

Credit Score—

It's important to use numbers that will look and feel familiar later, even though we won't use them the exact same way a credit bureau does, so keep her credit score between 500 and 800 points. 500 is the worst her credit can get, and 800 is the best. Although the real parameters are a little wider, this gives you an easy range to work within. Start her credit score at 700, which is considered good credit, and from that point on it's hers to do with as she will. I'm going to bullet some points here to make them easier to read:

- On a day-to-day basis you will work with her credit between the range of 500 to 750 points (you'll see how to get to 800 in the next section).

- All payments and credit affecting issues should be calculated on the 1st and 15th of each month.

- Every *successful* payment (or due date that passes when she makes all her payments) adds **5** points to her credit score up to a maximum of 750 points.

- Every *late* payment (three days or more) reduces her credit score 50 points.

- Every *missed* payment (a payment made after the next payment is due) reduces her credit score by 100 points. If she has two credit cards and misses both payments, you would lower her score by 200 points that period.

Making payments on time is good; missing payments is bad. When it gets down to crunch time, put late notices in her mailbox, but don't verbally remind her or try to force her to make payments on time. Remember she is learning how to be responsible and self-sufficient; having to work diligently for 40 weeks, and never being late on another payment, in order to repair the damage done by one missed payment, is a good way to teach her not to neglect her bills.

Revolving Credit—

Revolving credit is credit that is fluid rather than rigid. Credit cards are a form of revolving credit. Revolving credit is unlike installment credit, which is like the money loaned for a car loan. With installment credit, like a "secured" car loan, the money borrowed is used entirely on paying for the car. Also, with a car loan the payments are structured with a definitive start date and end date. Revolving credit, on the other hand, is a line of credit that can be used in increments, has no definitive end date and the payments are based on how much of it your son has used up to that point. If he uses a little, then he has to pay a little more back. When he uses a little more, then he pays a lot more back. Revolving credit is a cycle that goes on forever, like a revolving door. The most common type of revolving credit is, of course, the infamous credit card.

The top 50 points of her credit score is reserved for a few extra credit boosters. The first is revolving credit, or in our case, credit cards.

Credit Card Bonuses:

- Her first open credit card, which has to maintain a balance below 50% of its credit limit, gives her plus 10 points for a highest possible credit score of 760.

- Her second credit card (two total), which maintains a balance below 50% of its credit limit gives her another bonus of 10 points, for a highest possible credit score of 770.

- The maximum bonus for credit cards is 20 points, which is obtained by having two open credit cards, both maintaining balances below 50% of their respective credit limits.

Credit Card Penalties:

- If her first credit card balance goes over 50 % of it's credit limit, then she loses the 10 point bonus for that card **and** incurs a 10 point penalty, for a total possible credit score of 750, if her second credit card is still under 50% of its available credit limit. 770-20 (10 point loss of bonus and 10 point penalty) = 750 (highest possible score).

- If her second credit card balance goes over 50% of it's credit limit, then she loses the extra 10 points for that card **and** incurs another 10 point penalty, for a total possible credit score of 730 points. 750-20 (10 point loss of bonus and 10 point penalty) = 730 (highest possible score).

- The two potential 10 point bonuses for having credit cards with balances under 50% of their available credit limit only applies to her first and second credit cards. She will obtain no bonus for having a third credit card with a balance under 50% of it's credit limit, even if she is currently receiving no bonus because one or both of the first two credit cards have a balance above 50% of their limits.

- If she possesses more than two credit cards, then she will continue to receive 10 point penalties for every credit card that has a balance over 50% of its credit limit. So, if she opens six credit cards and they are all under 50 % of their limit, then her maximum credit score is 770. However, if four of her cards go over 50 percent of their respective limits, then her maximum credit score is 710 points. 770-(20 + 20 + 10 + 10) = 710.

Notice that even if your daughter has never missed a payment in her life, but she has four credit cards with balances over 50% of their credit limits, her credit score is seriously negatively impacted. In the real world a couple of credit cards held under 50% of their respective credit limits really does increase a person's credit score; likewise, maxed out credit cards really do have a negative impact on a person's credit score. In reality the scale is a sliding scale and it is much more complicated. Please be aware, too, that calculating a credit score in the real world is not as simple as in The Family Bank. The Family Bank credit system is not meant for you to be able to accurately calculate your real credit score; it's meant to be easy for you to use with The Family Bank, but also to teach your children lessons about controlling their credit scores that translate into useful real world knowledge.

Ideally, we want to teach our children to keep two open credit cards with their limits as high as the bank will allow, but with the balances on both cards well below 50% of each card's available credit limit, and hopefully closer to around 10% of the card's available credit limit. By maintaining open credit cards with high credit limits and low balances over an extended period of time, your daughter will be able to show creditors that she knows how to use credit responsibly, which will be reflected by her high credit score.

Also, just like in real life, the more credit cards she opens the lower the credit limit will be on each new card. In The Family Bank, if she is sixteen years old with good established credit, then she might have a primary credit card with a limit of $1,000 and a secondary card with a limit of $500. If she opens a third card, the limit will be $200, the next credit card will have a limit of $100, and so on. The more credit cards she has, the lower each card's limit will be and the harder it becomes to stay under 50% of the credit limit on each card.

Reality check: here is an overview on how revolving credit affects your real credit score. This is theory, not actual mathematical equations. Credit cards increase your credit score if they have a minimal balance on them of less than 10% of your total available credit limit. By having a high limit and a low balance, it shows creditors that you are financially responsible. Also, the longer your credit card is open, the better its impact on your credit score, because now it shows long-term financial responsibility on your part. I use 50% as the cutoff point in The Family Bank, where any balance over that has an adverse effect on her credit score. In reality, it's a sliding scale and the higher her balance creeps, the lower her score drops. But going above 50% of her credit limit is where she will start to truly notice adverse effects to her credit score. All in all, it's common to see her credit card balance push her credit score around within a 30 point window. Unless you happen to be a financial advisor or an accountant, though, I suggest you use the method I outlined above for The Family Bank. Remember, you are teaching the principles of revolving credit to your child, so don't stress yourself out too much with intricate details.

Secured Installment Credit—

Just as installment credit will increase your son's real credit score (as long it is kept current), so does it increase his Family Bank credit score.

So, now we will talk about secured installment credit. A secured loan is a loan from a creditor that is backed by something of value equal to the loan. An installment loan simply means that the loan is paid back in regular, usually equal installments. A common form of a secured installment loan is a car or home loan. Since the bank can't hold on to the actual car when they give a car loan, they hold the Title to the car instead. Obviously, holding the Title allows the bank to repossess the car if the person who took out the loan stops making payments.

In order to teach your children about secured installment credit as part of The Family Bank, you can use a New Bike Loan, an XBOX 360 Loan or a loan for absolutely anything, really; just create a Title for the item purchased.

Just like revolving credit, installment credit also has a positive effect on a person's credit score, as long as the loan payments are made on time. Therefore, just like in the Revolving Credit section, a secured installment Family Bank loan will increase your son's credit score by 10 points. The 10 point bonus is a one-time deal in The Family Bank, so if your son obtains a secured installment loan before he obtains credit cards, then upon successfully paying off his secured installment loan in full you will give his credit score a permanent 10 point bonus; thus his maximum credit score will increase to 760 points. (750 + 10 = 760) It's more likely, though, that your son will obtain a secured installment loan after he already has credit cards, so let's say your son has perfect Family Bank credit and he has two credit cards, both with balances less than 50% of their respective credit limits. All this being the case, your son will have a credit score of 780 points; 770 points for his credit cards plus 10 points for paying off his first secured installment loan.

The Family Bank gives only one bonus to your son's credit for installment loans, because installment credit is easy to understand and use in the real world. In order to keep the credit score numbers simple in The Family Bank, we only have to worry about one installment credit bonus. The best part about installment loans is that the total amount of money paid in interest is usually disclosed at the time of the signing of the loan. Therefore, the most dangerous aspect of secured installment loans, to most people, is not the interest but the introduction of a sizable monthly payment into their budget; having said that, I have to mention that some installment loans offer dangerous variable interest rates. In order to keep things simple for you, The Family Bank will never utilize variable interest rates, and in order to make sure your son does not get blind-sided by them in the real world, just teach him in a Weekly Meeting that they exist and that he needs to avoid them at all cost. Teach your son to seek out low interest fixed rate loans, never variable or adjustable rate loans.

Eventually, (about age sixteen), your son will also have to buy his bedroom from you. Yes, that is correct. He will buy his bedroom from you, the "Family Home Owner's Association" and just like in a real gated community, he will own his own bedroom.

Purchasing his bedroom is how your son will boost his Family Credit Score up that last 20 points. Upon making his very first payment on his new Bedroom Loan you will add a 20 point bonus to his credit score, basically just for having the loan. Your son owning his own bedroom shows stability, which is the reason for the credit boost. Therefore, if your son's credit is perfect and he has already obtained his other potential bonuses, then his credit will now be 800 points (780 for the other bonuses + 20 points for the Bedroom Loan). We will discuss the Bedroom Loan in more detail in Chapter 21—Loans.

So, why work so hard at getting his credit score up so high? Because he will have to have a Family Credit Score of 775 or better to be able to qualify for a Family Small Business Loan . . . and the plot thickens. We'll cover purchasing his bedroom versus renting his bedroom, and small business entrepreneurship in the latter chapters of this book. In short, his credit works between the scores of 500 and 750, with a total possible of 800 if he is able to maintain: two open credit cards with balances under 50 percent of their respective credit limits, a secured installment loan (like a Bike Loan) and a Bedroom Loan.

On a side note, you are never going to make him get a co-signer for any loan. The Family Bank teaches individual responsibility and accountability, so co-signers play no role here. As your son gets older, you will use your Weekly Meetings to fill in some of the gaps between the lessons of The Family Bank and the real world, like co-signers. By the time your son hits age eighteen, he will be so proficient using credit that he will scoff at the idea of needing a co-signer on his first real car loan; however, that is, of course, how the real world works. So, explain to him that The Family Bank has taught him the foundation of what he needs to know, but that there is always more to learn. You'll have to explain about Co-Signers, Bankruptcy, the Stock Market and anything else you can think of or that he asks you about in your Weekly Meetings.

You will find that The Family Bank focuses on teaching lessons about personal financial responsibility, and leaves out certain realities like Bankruptcy, in order to teach these lessons. The real world financial systems have built-in safeguards against banks losing their money, but those safeguards do not help you to teach personal responsibility, so we sacrifice a little realism in The Family Bank when it comes to working with credit, in order to reach our desired outcome, which is having children who will never need or use those safeguards.

Chapter 22

Interest

Hopefully, the earlier example of the candy at lunch gave your son a cursory understanding of what interest is, but it's also imperative he understands how important and necessary it is to his financial well-being. It is also imperative that upon closing his Family Bank accounts when he moves out, that he fully, fully understands that interest is what makes or breaks personal wealth and financial stability.

Interest is the arsenic that creditors will try to feed your son over the course of his life that will degrade and/or kill his financial success. I'm not saying that interest is evil, it's not; in fact it is necessary in order for people to enjoy the staples of life, like buying a home for their family and a car to get to work. Without interest no one would lend money and without lenders we wouldn't be able to open businesses big or small, or put our kids through college. So, here we come back around again to the importance of balance and moderation.

Creditors try to downplay the impact of interest as much as possible in order to part us from our money. Car dealerships talk about, "Where do you want your monthly payment to be?" never "Where would you like your interest rate to be?" So, your job is to teach your son the true impact of interest before he hits the real world.

As you are well aware, the greatest danger regarding interest is also its greatest strength, which is the fact that it **compounds**. The idea behind compounding interest is so simple and so benign on the surface that the power of compounding interest almost always goes unrecognized by the average person. In fact, many people hear about the benefits of compounding interest when it comes to saving for retirement and do a good job of saving money early on in life, but they don't truly understand that credit card debt compounds the same way an IRA or retirement fund does. Many people who started saving money early find themselves, in their thirties or forties, so far in credit card debt that they have to withdraw their retirement savings to pay off those credit cards. Therefore, there is a difference between your son hearing that interest is powerful, and your son understanding how interest works for him and how it works against him.

When a person puts money into his retirement or savings account, but maintains a balance over 10% of his credit card's limit, it shows that he has heard about the power of compounding interest, but doesn't really understand it. Your job is to teach your children about the power of compounding interest, so that they can internalize it, respect it and then utilize it for themselves. This may sound like a lesson for a Weekly Meeting, but unfortunately it's not that simple; it's actually the main reason for opening The Family Bank and it's a lesson that takes years to understand and to master.

The Family Bank

So, during your "interest" Weekly Meeting, you will, in fact, explain to your son that creditors calculate interest charges more often than he might expect. Some creditors calculate interest annually, some monthly and some daily, and the more frequently interest is compounded the harder it works against him. You'll also give him the example that you have heard a hundred times: if you put $1000 on a credit card that has a 12% interest rate, the credit card company is going to calculate the interest charges every month and add them to the balance. So after one month, the creditor will add $10 to your balance in interest charges; one month later they will charge you interest again on your original $1000 dollars, plus they will charge you interest on the interest charge from the month before. Like I said before, your son will hear your example and just like everyone else, he'll think "Great, who cares?"

Getting kids to understand this lesson on compounding interest is extremely difficult, obviously, or you wouldn't be reading this right now. Every generation, the cycle continues like this: adults tell kids about the evils of compounding interest, kids don't listen and/or don't understand, kids grow up and lose untold fortunes to compounding interest, reckless kids become adults who learned hard lessons from experience, then these new adults tell kids about the evils of compounding interest (and we're back to stage one). Well, The Family Bank is going to break that vicious cycle for your family.

The ability to teach our children these lessons about interest is why we want to keep interest in The Family Bank as simple as possible. People, especially kids, tend to "tune out" anything that is too complicated for them to understand. So we have to make the long—term effects of interest dramatic and tangible to our kids, which means turning the long-term consequences of interest into something your son has to think about and deal with on a daily basis. As adults, we get our interest rate on our home mortgage when we sign the loan, but then we never think about that venomous interest rate again; it's just too painful. In order to learn about the effects of interest, kids need to be reminded about it on a daily basis, so again we will turn to the trusty Whiteboard.

Even if you take shortcuts on every other aspect of The Family Bank, it's important that you follow this section "by the numbers". The entire purpose of running The Family Bank is to prevent your kids from getting into debt over their heads when they turn eighteen years old, and the only way for them to "pre-learn" that lesson is for you to teach your kids, through The Family Bank, the dangers of interest and how easily revolving credit will take the reins of your son's financial future right out of his hands.

Displaying Interest—

The Whiteboard gives you and your account holders a constant visual reminder of the state of all his accounts, so it makes sense that everything we focus on in The Family Bank is going to have a place on it. The Whiteboard will list: each of your son's accounts along with his current balance; his lines of credit with their current balances; and his credit score will sit up there along with the monthly interest rate of each line of credit *and* somewhere up there you will *keep the total amount of interest he has paid on each line of credit along with a running total of how much interest he has paid on all his lines of credit totaled together.* This "all interest" total should become pretty substantial by the time your son graduates from high school. This running total will help drive

The Family Bank

home the point about how much damage interest will do to his overall financial health. If you were to see that total for all your own personal accounts you'd probably get chest pains! I just calculated the monthly interest I pay on just my home, cars, student loans and credit cards at almost $1100 per month and I've been paying about that much for at least 150 months! Think about that for a minute . . . let me help you . . . I've paid at least $165,000.00 over the past thirteen years, and I've only averaged the same annual salary as the average American.

Paying interest or "buying money" is the heart of our financial system; there is no doubt about it. Credit companies try to minimize customers' negative reactions to paying interest by spreading it out and diverting your attention away from it, so get it out there for your kids to see. Once your kids learn how substantial an amount of money it is that they will lose during their lives to paying interest, hopefully swiping that credit card will sting a little. Like we talked about earlier, secured installment credit is necessary in order to buy those larger items like a home and a car, but the idea is to get his credit score high enough to keep those secured credit interest rates low, and also to not acquire large amounts of credit card and unsecured, high interest debt. Forget a penny: $165 thousand dollars saved, could have been $165 thousand dollars earned!

Chapter 23

Credit Cards

So, your daughter has a job and has established an employment history, and you have thoroughly explained to her the concepts of credit, her credit score and interest; now it's time to have her apply for her first credit card. If you are thinking that ten years old is too young for a child to have a credit card, I assure you it's not. We are aiming for 10,000 hours of practice, remember?

During these young and formative years, kids are often highly judgmental and equally impressionable. Kids see life as being far more black-and-white than adults do. Take advantage of these years to let your daughter experiment with her credit card and come to the conclusion on her own that credit cards can cause severe damage to her finances when they are used irresponsibly. Once she has processed that idea into her psyche it will be very difficult to change it later in life. People's values are like molded plastic; they can only be molded once and only in the very beginning. Once your daughter's values have taken shape, they can sometimes bend a little, but not much, and they always bounce back. Your children are impressionable, so leave the right impression the first time; compounding interest is a force to be respected. Teach your daughter to use interest for her benefit (saving for retirement) and to never let it be used against her.

Utilizing Interest in The Family Bank—

Normal credit card interest rates run from 6% to about 35%, so we will work in the 10 to 20% (*monthly, not yearly*) range in The Family Bank. These numbers will "look" familiar later on, even though they truly hit home somewhere around 200% interest annually; it just gets the point across so much more convincingly!

When your daughter gets her first credit card, she has to have an actual plastic credit card. So contact your bank and ask them to open a prepaid credit card with your daughter's name on it. Some banks allow you to open a prepaid card with your daughter's name on it, some banks will only let you open a prepaid credit card with your own name on it . . . roll with it. Figure out what you can do and make it work for you. Ideally though, you will be able to get a prepaid card in her name. The actual credit line that your daughter is taking out is through you, The Family Bank. This means that you have to front the money for the prepaid card; after all, you are the bank and your money is supplying her credit. The Family Bank is a pretend and yet a very real institution. Under no circumstances will your child pay the prepayment money for the credit card. If she does that, then in reality it has become a debit card, because it's all her money to begin with.

As the CEO, you are responsible for the financial health of The Family Bank, so when you accept an application from your daughter for a credit card, take the time to really think about her financial situation and then determine if she is qualified, and what the terms will be. The bottom line, though, is that if your daughter has a job and no extenuating circumstances, then you will approve her credit card application, just like in real life.

If your daughter is happy with the terms you gave her for her new credit card, she doesn't understand how compounding interest works yet, and you are about to reach that special part of her life when you are going to teach her the hard lessons about credit cards. If you think it's hard to stay on top of a credit card with a 15% annual interest rate, just wait until your daughter is trying to manage a 15% *monthly* interest rate.

I won't go into painstaking detail about how to use credit cards in The Family Bank. Just make sure that during the first few years she has it, she only uses it when you are present. Your daughter will **not** use her credit card the same way as her debit card, by simply telling you she wants to use it to charge something and then you buy it. She needs to develop the full appreciation for how easy it is to use credit cards, so you will have her ring up credit card transactions, herself; however, you will still notate the transaction in your day planner and transfer it to your journal later. After your daughter has been using her credit card for a few years, and she's around fourteen years old, you can let her use her credit cards when you are not with her, but she will have to turn her receipts in to The Family Bank every evening for your records. Now that we've nailed down how to use the credit card, let's take a look at the parameters of credit cards within The Family Bank:

- Her first credit card should start at 15% interest (with her credit hovering around 700, like we discussed earlier).

- If she is five days late on a single payment the interest rate permanently jumps to 20% and she is assessed a $30 late fee.

- For a new credit card: 500 to 650 credit score equals 20% interest rate, 655 to 745 credit score equals 15% interest rate and 750 to 800 credit score equals 10% interest rate.

- The interest rate will never go down on an existing credit card regardless of how her Family Credit Score changes (no variable rates either). In order for her to get a better interest rate she will have to apply for a better card. After all, when was the last time your credit card company called you and asked you if they could lower your interest rate?

- The first credit card limit should be *four times her monthly wages* rounded down. Let's say she has a typical job cleaning the house and making $15 a week at age ten, so she makes about $60 dollars a month or $240 every four months, which would make her credit limit $200.

- When she applies for a second credit card, as long as she has the same salary, her credit limit should be $100, even though the interest rate may be better if she has a better credit score. Remember that each additional credit card she applies for will have a credit limit of about half the amount of the last credit card she obtained, rounded down.

- Finally, you will calculate the minimum "bi-monthly" payment to be 10% of the balance on the credit card, after you have added her interest charge. Remember that your daughter has to make two payments per month, so one week before each payment is due you will create a bill for her and put it in your outbox (basically your daughter's inbox). Balance + half her monthly interest rate charge = new balance. 10% of new balance = minimum payment due.

- Formula for 10% interest charge: Balance x 1.05 = New Balance

- Formula for 15% interest charge: Balance x 1.075 = New Balance

- Formula for 20% interest charge: Balance x 1.1 = New Balance

- Formula for Minimum Payment: New Balance x 0.1 = Minimum Payment

For example, let's say your daughter still makes $15 per week and has a credit card with a 15% interest rate and a $200 credit limit, and of course she maxes out her credit card. One week before her payment is due, you will sit down and create a bill, so you will have to use the formulas above. First, you have to add the interest charge, so you'll take her balance of $200 and multiply it by 1.075 (which is 7.5%, or half of her monthly interest rate), because the bill is for half a month. $200 multiplied by 1.075 is $215, so she had an interest charge of $15, or exactly one weeks' worth of work. Her minimum monthly payment will be $215 multiplied by 0.1, which equals $21.50. After making a payment of $21.50 for that bi-monthly period, her new balance will be $215 minus $21.50, which equals $193.50.

The above example illustrates the point that with a 15% interest rate on a maxed-out credit card, your daughter will be making a minimum monthly payment that will be a little more than a weeks' worth of work for her. At 10% interest, the payment will be just about a week of work and at 20% interest her minimum payment will be around a week and a half worth of work during a two week period. This amount will be impossible to deal with when she has other bills, such as paying her rent. In the worst case scenario of a maxed-out credit card with a 20% interest rate, your daughter will have to use up her savings until she eventually falls behind on her payments. You may have also noticed that at 20% interest, your daughter's minimum monthly payment will be equal to her interest charge, so her balance will never decrease, which is no accident! Eventually, your daughter will learn to keep her credit card balance below 50% of the credit limit, so she will maintain good credit and have credit cards at 10% interest. When all these stars finally align, her bi-monthly payment won't be higher than $10.50, which is manageable when her pay is $30 for the same period of time. Also, don't forget that those interest charges are profit for The Family Bank!

Recovering from Credit Card Mishaps—

Once your daughter is armed with the knowledge that you provide her in the Weekly Meetings, and she is equipped with a credit card in hand, she is going to make all great decisions right from the beginning, right? Umm . . . no. Credit cards are what financially destroy most Americans, so don't expect that with a little pep talk from you, your ten-year-old is going to hit the ground running, and making *none* of the mistakes you and I made when we were eighteen years old and swipe happy! Remember the lessons learned will come from experience, so don't get upset when she maxes out her credit card in the first month. Play by all The Family Bank rules of credit score, interest rates and credit limits and let her work through all the problems that she creates. Don't limit, "as a parent", what she is allowed to buy with her money, as the entire purpose of The Family Bank is that it *is* her money! Now let me reiterate: if she spends all her money on candy, or clothing you told her was inappropriate, you don't have to let her eat it or wear them! You just have to let her buy them. If you want to confiscate the candy or the mini-skirt your ten-year-old bought, and tell her that you'll give it back to her when she's 30, that's perfectly fine.

If the worst case scenario does happen, and your daughter immediately maxes out her credit card and within two months has gotten to the point where she is missing payments and absolutely can't make ends meet, then it's time for some Weekly Meeting credit counseling. When you start counseling her regarding credit, unlike real credit counseling agencies, the one thing you will never do is make payments *for* her. You will guide her, but she will always have complete control over all her accounts. So, the actual credit counseling will consist of two parts: explaining how she got to the point she is at, and what she needs to do to fix the situation.

First, walk her through her records. Show her the interest charges from every bill and ask her if the stuff she purchased using her credit card was really worth the hassle of trying to pay it all back. Point out to your daughter that since she maxed out her credit card she hasn't had the money to buy anything new, and that the balance does not go down very much with each minimum payment she makes. Then show her that if she had just saved the same amount that she was wasting on credit card payments, she could have saved the original $200 she spent on her credit card in about twenty weeks; however by purchasing the items on her credit card she will be paying it back for a year, and she'll end up paying about twice as much!

The important points to stress during the "how we got here" Weekly Meeting are these: if she had saved her money, then she would not have had the thing she wanted right away, but when she was done saving up she would have been able to buy the item she wanted and she would not have had to continue to make the extra credit card payments for another five months. Also, during the time she was saving her money, she would have actually had money in her account, accruing interest, which she could have used in case of an emergency.

This point about having money in her account for emergencies is another vitally important point that your daughter is going to learn the hard way, unfortunately. The first time your daughter has to miss horseback riding summer camp, because she is in credit card debt over her head and can't pay for the lessons, will be extremely painful for you to watch; but you cannot break down and bail her out under any circumstances. Be strong! Your daughter will only learn the important lessons by internalizing the consequences of making bad financial decisions. Besides, she still has years and years ahead of her to make up those horseback riding lessons. Conversely, if you want your daughter to go to summer camp and she has been making all good financial decisions, but you realize you have not been paying her enough money to be able to afford the riding lessons, then you will have to either give her a good bonus (if you don't have enough time before summer), or convince her to apply for a new job that pays better (if you do have enough time). Hopefully, your daughter will learn a hard lesson about managing credit cards the first time around; if not, then you'll both end up repeating the entire process over again, which is perfectly fine.

Now that your daughter knows how she got into credit card debt over her head and that she can't get out, you'll have to help her fix it. Do this by explaining to her that because her credit score is still good (have this talk before she ruins her credit score), she can use something she owns as collateral and apply to The Family Bank for a low interest secured installment loan. The installment loan will lower her payments to something manageable and it will have an end date, unlike her credit card. Then have her cancel her credit card and turn it in to you. She will survive this "near disaster" with her credit card and learn some valuable lessons about not getting in credit card debt over her head.

Explain to your daughter that by making her payments on the secured installment loan, she will continue to build her credit score, and then after the loan is paid off in full she will have to apply to The Family Bank for another credit card with a better interest rate. If she is hesitant to apply for a new credit card after this ordeal, explain to her how credit cards are necessary and how she can't book a hotel room, rent a car, buy plane tickets, shop online or do anything else that requires a credit card . . . without a credit card. One of the major keys to financial success is to maintain two good credit cards and to be responsible with them, not to avoid credit cards or pretend like they don't exist.

Maintain Good Records—

Keep in mind that the balance on her credit card is not going to exactly match the amount she has charged on her prepaid card, because you can't put a charge on her card for the Family Bank interest accrued. So if she has a credit limit of $200, and she has spent $100 this month, then on your online account it will show that she still has $100 left on the prepaid card; however, you will know that due to The Family Bank 15% interest charge, she is only allowed to spend $85 more before the credit card is maxed out.

You obviously have to keep accurate records of her balances and transactions in your credit notebook, and if she does go over her credit limit you will have to charge her the typical $30 over-the-limit charge. As your daughter makes payments on her credit card at The Family Bank, you will transfer the principle portion of the payment amounts onto her credit card through your bank (minus your Family Bank interest charge, which The Family Bank will keep), so she will be able to continue to use the actual credit card. If your daughter has a balance of $200 on her credit card and her interest rate is 15%, then just like we calculated earlier, her payment to The Family Bank will $21.50. You will keep the $15 interest charge and apply the principle of $6.50 to her credit card, thus bringing her credit card balance down to $193.50. When all is said and done, don't forget to write the total interest she has now paid up on the whiteboard.

Rebuilding—

Even with all your guidance and wisdom, there is a good chance that your daughter will make mistakes and get into trouble with The Family Bank that you will not be able to prevent. Credit cards or revolving credit is most likely where your daughter is going to destroy her Family Bank credit score, so let me give you an idea you can teach in a Weekly Meeting to help your daughter rebuild her credit score after it hits rock bottom.

She can improve her credit score by taking out another loan and paying it off over the natural life of the loan. Wait . . . w-h-a-t? She'll be confused, because how can she get another loan when her Family Bank credit is a shiny 500? Well, start with her giving you (the Bank) collateral worth $50 to put toward a $50 loan (an actual $50 works best), which any bank would underwrite, no matter what her credit score is, because it's 100% secured. Then tell her to put the $50 of loan money into a dedicated savings account; don't spend it. Then, every other week on the payment due date she'll take $5 out of her dedicated savings account, using the money she borrowed to pay back her secured installment loan payment of $5 per week. After she has made eleven payments (not ten, due to interest), she will have successfully run the full term of the loan and paid it off in full. Once she pays off the loan, she gets her original $50 that she put down as collateral back, and her only out-of-pocket expense was the $5 she paid in interest on the loan. It is a small price to pay for bringing her credit score up 55 points. Eleven "on time" payments worth five credit points each = 55 points. Now she can start the process over again, and repeat it as many times as is necessary, to get her credit score back to 750 points, or at least 655 points, so she can get a credit card with a 15% interest rate. Never encourage your daughter to open a credit card with a 20% interest rate; rather, encourage her to build her credit enough to get a better credit card.

So, you have reported the successful loan payoff information to The Family Credit Bureau and raised her credit score back up again. In the end, she learned and utilized the tools of the adult system and she felt some of the pressure of making financial decisions, but simultaneously you helped her develop her knowledge and self-confidence and gave her valuable tools she probably wouldn't have learned otherwise until it's too late.

Chapter 24

Loans

Loans, just like credit cards, require your son to fill out a Family Bank loan application and his approval will be based on his income, credit score and work history. The biggest difference between credit cards and loans is that his loans will be secured. You can add unsecured installment loans (signature loans) to The Family Bank later on if you feel the urge. Based on all the general Family Bank guidelines, unsecured installment loans should be pretty self-explanatory, so I won't go into detail regarding unsecured loans or signature loans. I don't recommend unsecured loans because they are unnecessary and incur tremendous interest fees. Interest on unsecured installment loans is about double the rate of interest on secured installment loans. You will often see car loans at around 5% and signature loans at around 10%. Needless to say, the secured installment loan will be the most common loan you will deal with in The Family Bank. Besides, if your child defaults on his loan, then you have to have something you can repossess, or you're not teaching him accountability.

How much money should your son qualify for? What is his collateral worth? If he wants a secured loan for a new bike, it's easy; he puts the new bike up as collateral for the loan, and he's approved. Worried he'll get in over his head? That's okay, what lesson could he really learn if he never had to bring himself back from the brink of disaster? I've been there and I'll bet you have, too; and do you know who never denied me for a loan, even when it was too much for me to handle? My bank. He needs to learn on his own how to budget his money and where his financial limits are, so don't waste a second of your time trying to calculate your son's debt-to-income ratio. It's up to him to figure it out on his own. Besides, after you make one repossession, he'll never ask you again, "Why is a budget so important anyway?" A question I asked myself for the first twenty years of my life and then never again since.

Secured installment loans will work like this:

- You will calculate the interest rate similar to the way you did for the credit cards, but with lower interest. A credit score of 500 to 650 = 15% interest, 655 to 745 = 10% interest and 750 to 800 = 5% interest.

- To calculate his secured loan payments just add the interest to the total of the loan and then divide by 24 payments. For simplicity's sake, you will not compound the interest on secured installment loans.

- Formula for 5%: Loan Amount x 1.05 = Total loan amount

- Formula for 10%: Loan Amount x 1.1 = Total loan amount

- Formula for 15%: Loan Amount x 1.15 = Total loan amount

- Formula for bi-monthly payment: Total loan amount / 24 = Payment amount

For example, if he wants to buy a bike that costs $200, and his credit score is 700, then his interest rate will be 10%. $200 plus 10% = $220. All your secured loans will be for **one** year, or 24 bi-monthly payments due on the 1st and 15th of every month. $220 divided by 24 payments = $9.17 per payment. You will then send him an approval letter that you will generate from The Family Bank letterhead that states the following:

> *"This loan is for a* (describe the bike, make, model and year), *for which said bike Title will be held as collateral and will be returned to* (your son's name) *upon repayment in full of this loan in accordance with the terms set forth.*
>
> *The terms of the loan will be for an amount of $220 paid over one year or 24 payments of $9.17 due on the 1st and 15th of each month starting one month from the current date and at an interest rate of 10 percent."*

The first time your son expresses interest (not that kind of interest) in a new bike or something of the sort, it will be time for your Weekly Meeting on secured installment loans. I'll bet you are getting ready to skim this part, so I'll summarize it for you! At your Weekly Meeting you'll have to explain to him the difference between unsecured and secured debt, which is the use of collateral, and explain that "collateral" means that whatever you use to "secure" the loan you still get to use, but the bank technically owns it until the loan is fully repaid. When the secured loan is paid off in full, your son will get the "Title" to his item

The Family Bank

back and he will then technically own it. Your son can secure a loan with anything that has value to The Family Bank, to include objects like a bike, television or video game system, or even cash. Problems arise only if your son stops making payments on his loan (misses two payments). Should that happen, the bank will come and take possession of the item he used as collateral, which is repossession.

If your son misses a payment it will negatively impact his credit score, but if he misses two payments, then The Family Bank will repossess the item and only give it back when he gets current on his loan. If your son misses four payments in a row, then the bank will "foreclose" on his loan, which means The Family Bank will terminate your son's loan and sell the item used as collateral to someone else, in order to use the money to pay off his loan. If your son has an item repossessed, his credit score will drop 200 points or to 500, whichever comes first. If your son misses four payments and The Family Bank has to foreclose on his loan, then his credit score will drop to 500 and he will lose all bonuses he previously earned. After a foreclosure your son will have to rebuild his credit from scratch using the "secured installment loan" method we discussed earlier.

Using a foreclosure system for every secured loan (even for a bike or a video game console) works well in The Family Bank, because you don't want to be forced to sell your son's bike (after repossession) just because he missed two payments. Treat all secured loans like real life home mortgages, so that you build in that "one . . . two . . . two-and-a-half . . . two-and-three-quarters . . ." countdown, before you are forced to sell an expensive item. If your son misses four payments in row, then do what you have to do and go sell his bike. But your son being forced to look at his repossessed bike for a month after the original repossession, and not be able to ride it, is where you will drive home your lesson.

We discussed using the item being purchased as the collateral for a secured loan, but that does not always have to be the case. If the holidays roll around and Mr. Reckless doesn't have enough money saved up to buy his family gifts, then he will have to take out a secured loan that does not use the item purchased as the collateral. Again, you can implement signature loans into your Family Bank, but I prefer not to because it is unnecessary and nothing is at stake for non-repayment of the loan. So, Mr. Reckless uses his video game console as collateral and submits an application to you for a secured loan. You grant the loan and voilà, he is off shopping and hopefully you didn't just buy yourself a Nintendo, an XBOX or a Playstation.

The Bedroom Mortgage—

The biggest secured loan that your son is likely to face in The Family Bank is the Bedroom Mortgage. The Bedroom Mortgage is the rough equivalent of a real world Home Mortgage. You don't want to bring up the Bedroom Mortgage too early to your renters, as it should be something they strive for only when they are ready. If your son starts working at around age nine and begins renting his room at around age eleven, then logically you should introduce the Bedroom Mortgage at around age thirteen. This is not to say that his credit or employment will sustain a Bedroom Mortgage that early, but by age fourteen he will hopefully have secured a good enough job with The Family Bank, and raised his credit score to the necessary 750 point minimum, for a Bedroom Loan. You will calculate the payments for the Bedroom

Mortgage the same way you calculate any other secured loan, except you will divide the loan into 60 monthly payments instead of the usual 24 bi-monthly payments. Also you will use a flat interest rate of 10%.

You want the Bedroom Mortgage to cost a bit more than the rent he was paying, so in order to figure out the selling price of the Bedroom you will have to work it out backwards. If he was paying $400 per month in rent, then start with his current rent payment of $400 and multiply that amount by 60 months (the life of the loan), which equals $24,000. You will list the Bedroom for sale for $24,000. Once your son is approved for the Bedroom Mortgage, you will add a simple 10% to the total, which on $24,000 brings the total paid over the life of the loan up to $26,400. Divide the total with interest by the 60 months and you have the total monthly payment including interest, in this case $440. By doing the cost of the bedroom this way, it becomes apparent that he is paying an extra $40 a month in interest on his loan, a painful little reminder that borrowing money isn't free.

Side note: The method above is not how mortgage interest is calculated in the real world; however, we want to keep The Family Bank as simple and easy to use as possible. In the end your son will learn to control compounding interest charges via The Family Bank credit card, and he'll learn to budget loan payments using The Family Bank secured installment loans. The only lessons we are aiming to teach with the Bedroom Mortgage are a sense of adult responsibility and the necessity of maintaining a good job in order to be able to afford the things he wants.

Your son might not be super enthusiastic about paying an extra $40 for the same room he was already living in, so you have to make the idea of room ownership more enticing. All teenagers want privacy, and so do all adults, really, so guess what he is going to buy for that extra $40 per month; yup, privacy. When he owns his own room, you will no longer be his landlord, which means his room will no longer be subjected to regular inspections. If this sounds less than appealing to you, keep in mind that you can always ask him if you can come into his room to talk and hang out, and then take a gooood look around while you're in there. You can also make cleaning his room a part of many of the jobs he applies for, thus making his room subject to job performance inspection. If you're still not convinced, then look at it this way; if you don't sell him his bedroom, then he will just put up a big "Keep Out!" sign anyway, and continually demand privacy. At least this way you preempt the sign and make his privacy something he has to earn from you, instead of something he has to take from you.

Also, keep in mind that the property your teenager is purchasing is in a "gated community" (your front door) and thus he is buying it from the "Family Home Owner's Association", which will have a list of set rules that the owner has to follow, or penalties will be levied against him: it has to be kept clean, he can't alter it in any major way without written consent, and anything else you may want to add. A word of caution, though, the rules that go along with the bedroom purchase cannot be unrelated to the room, so you can't penalize his loan or reposes his bedroom for breaking curfew, as curfew is a job for Mom the parent, not Mom the CEO.

Reality check:

Just because you call yourself The Family Bank doesn't mean you are automatically made of money and are capable of extending thousand dollar lines of credit. I get this. This is a substantial issue and there is no easy way around it. First, just because Mr. Reckless submits a loan application that he is well qualified for, does not mean you have to process the loan and dole out the funds within 24 hours. If you can generate the funds to extend him the credit line in three weeks, then the loan will just have to take three weeks to get processed. If you **do** have enough money saved up to cover all your children's credit endeavors, then great, skip ahead; but if you don't have that money lying around, then keep reading.

If your oldest child is eight years old when you open your Family Bank, then open a separate account for yourself and label it your children's college fund (you should have already done that, anyway). Put at least $20 per month in this account. If $20 sounds like too much, well . . . suck it up; you owe your children that much. $20 a month is only $240 a year, which is not close to being enough money to put anyone through college; however, it is enough money to run The Family Bank flawlessly. How does The Family Bank equate to college? Not everyone has the means to pay for their children's full tuition for four years of college, but the prevailing idea seems to be, "if I can't save enough money for *all* his college, then I won't save *any* money for his college and he'll have to figure out a way to pay for it himself". There is a middle ground, though. Save enough money to teach your kids everything they need to know about being financially successful, by saving enough money to run your Family Bank credit system. If you can teach your kids how to be financially savvy, then at least repaying their college loans will come easily to them. You may not be able to give your kids all the money they need for the rest of their lives, but you can give them the tools they will need for the rest of their financial lives. Besides, if you open The Family Bank when your son is eight years old, and run it for 10 years so he closes out all his accounts at age eighteen, then you will have saved about $2,400 in his "college fund" that you were using for his credit lines; add this $2,400 to whatever your son was able to save on his own over those ten years and you will find that he has far more money for college that you ever dreamed you would be able to save.

Do it.

Checking and savings accounts, a job, credit cards, secured installment loans, bills, rent, room ownership . . . what else could The Family Bank possibly have to offer?

SECTION VII

Entrepreneurship

Every lesson forged over the life of The Family Bank will ideally culminate in your daughter starting up, managing and generating real profit from her own business. At about age sixteen, your daughter will have all the tools necessary to manage the financial aspects of a Family Bank Business. At this point it is all about putting her knowledge to good use. Starting up her own business will test her ability to manage and control her money, create a sophisticated budget, apply for necessary lines of credit and to generate and present a business plan. Every child is unique and different, so the best Mentor you can be is one who supports and gives counsel only when you are asked for it, and then sits back and watches her work her magic.

Following are a few points you absolutely have to internalize before you talk to your daughter, in a Weekly Meeting, about starting her own business. First, this is your daughter's Family Business, not yours. She will have her own ideas for her business and she will want to try out her ideas on her own. Some of her ideas are obviously not going to work, but that is for her to learn and not for you to tell her. Think back to your childhood for a moment, and remember a time when you had an idea that you tried, but it didn't work. Now think back to a time when someone told you not to do something because it was a bad idea. Which one of those memories sticks with you, even today, and which of those scenarios did you find annoying and dismiss immediately? Everyone learns better from experience than from other people telling them what to do, so just like every other section of The Family Bank, your children will stumble through this section using trial and error.

Second, starting up her own business is not meant to be a confidence builder; it just is what it is, a learning tool. It might succeed or it might fail. The purpose of your daughter starting her own business is to get the first time out of the way. The first time you do anything, whether it's the first day on a new job, the first time flying on an airplane alone or the first time you try to run your own business, the first time is always stressful and requires overcoming a tremendous mental hurdle. Running a business at sixteen years old gets the first time out of the way at a young age, and does it in a way that is relatively stress free, where your daughter's entire livelihood isn't on the line. Whether running her own business ends up to be her calling in life, or just a once in a lifetime deal, at least she'll get the opportunity to try it.

Lastly, her businesses success or failure says absolutely nothing about your success or failure as a Mentor, as CEO of The Family Bank or as a parent. Disassociate yourself from her business venture and you'll see that the entire experience will turn out to be a great one.

Remember that your role in your daughter's Family Business is to be there to answer her questions and to help her with all the financial "stuff". Her business is truly a test of the tools she's learned from The Family Bank; it's not a test of her ingenuity, resourcefulness or entrepreneurial spirit. If she tries to ask you too many questions about the business itself, like "what kind of business should I run?" don't answer the questions directly, just help guide her by posing counter questions like, "what are you interested in?"

Chapter 25

Starting Up the Family Bank Small Business

Now let's get down to "business". The first step for your son starting up his own Family Business is to figure out what he wants to do. There is no limit to the possibilities: dog walking, running a car wash, making and selling t-shirts, baby-sitting, cleaning trusted neighbors' and friends' houses, buying yard sale items and selling them on the Internet, etc. The possibilities are endless and anything he can think of should be thoroughly discussed and given serious consideration.

To kick this off, your son is going to go to The Family Bank, choose a name for his new company and fill out an application for a business license and Articles of Organization to create his own Limited Liability Company. That's right, he needs his own LLC. The only way for your son to feel truly in charge of his Family Business is to be the CEO of his own company. The application process should take about a week to get approved and cost Mr. Entrepreneur about $250, or however much you decide to charge him. Starting his own LLC is not mandatory, but it makes a nice segue from thinking about finances from the perspective of working for someone else, to assuming the legal responsibility of working for himself.

I'm guessing you are probably not an expert at starting up your own LLC, so instead of killing yourself, just Google "LLC" and grab the sample paperwork from the Internet. You don't have to be an expert, just getting paperwork and letting your son fill it out is a huge step to introducing him to the process of owning his own business. The paperwork is actually very short and easy to fill out. I've said it before, but it's worth repeating . . . he is only sixteen years old and what we are doing here is an introduction into the real world, so don't get too bogged down in the details. You're just giving him a taste of the real world here.

Having said that, if your son has been running his own Family Business for a few months and it is amazingly successful, don't be afraid to go online and fill out the requisite paperwork for real, and go through the process to really file it. The more experience he gets, the better. But assuming we are starting from the beginning, now that Mr. Entrepreneur has his own Family Business, he needs to get it off the ground and running. The bottom line is that your son will apply to the Family Bank to create his LLC, he will apply for the necessary city permits and business licenses to run his business, and then he'll apply for his first Family Bank Small Business Loan.

The next step is for Mr. Entrepreneur to submit his application for a Family Bank Small Business Loan, even if he already has plenty of money to cover the start-up costs himself. I truly hope that convincing him to fill out an application for a small business loan is the most difficult concept you will have to sell to your son during the entire life of The Family Bank. Most kids don't have $20 to their name by the time they turn eighteen years old; in fact, regardless of how wealthy their parents are or how long they have been working, most kids do not have $20 of their own in their own savings account. But by the time your son is sixteen years old he will have thousands saved if you have been running The Family Bank since he was eight, which brings us back to his application for a Family Bank Small Business Loan.

You have been teaching your son for eight years to avoid excess interest charges and to save money, so don't be surprised if he is reluctant to take out a Family Bank Small Business Loan when he has ten times the necessary cash on hand. Explain to him that our financial system rewards those people who have strong personal finances and who keep their business ventures separate from their personal finances. Also, in the real world he might have $50k saved up, but if he wants to open a restaurant he is going to need to come up with something in the neighborhood of $300k to $500k, so learning how to get a small business loan and/or financial backers is a necessary skill.

When your son goes to start a business he will open a separate account for his business (his LLC) and he won't transfer any of his own money into that account. In a sense he really will need a loan, because his business account will have zero dollars in it at start-up. Of course, the Family Bank will only lend Mr. Entrepreneur $100 no matter how qualified he is, so he is going to need to find financial backing for his start-up LLC from another source.

Chapter 26

Creating the Business Proposal

Research—

Once your daughter has figured out what type of business she wants to run and has done the appropriate paperwork to get it started, the next step is to do some research. The research portion will differ greatly from one Family Bank to another, depending on the type of Family Business, but the principle is always the same: she has to figure out what she can charge for her services, determine the level of demand for her services, calculate her start-up and maintenance costs and most importantly, find out if she needs any permits or licenses for the business she is starting up.

For example, let's say your daughter wants to start a dog walking business. Her research might include using your block as a sample area and taking you with her during a Weekly Meeting to knock on every door on the block. She will do all the talking and explain to each neighbor that she is starting up a dog walking business and ask the following questions. "Do they have a dog? Would they be interested in hiring a dog walker? How much would they be willing to pay for the service? How often would they like their dogs walked? Are there any other services they would be interested in for their dogs, like dog sitting during a vacation, bathing them or anything else?"

Once your daughter has finished her sample research area and collected all of her data, you will help her to inquire from the City if she needs any permits or licenses for her business. Once you have all the information you will use a Weekly Meeting to help her create a business plan. Her business plan can be on a computer (projected onto a screen or presented straight off the monitor) or it can be on paper (either typed or hand written). What's important is the planning and coordination that goes into the presentation, more than the format of the presentation itself. The presentation will include:

- All the sample data

- The sample size

- Estimated income potential of the business, based upon extending the sample size area to the actual work area

- A breakdown of her calculated expenses to include the cost of the business license or permits

Let's say that in our example your block only has two neighbors with dogs, each has one dog and both would like their dog walked three times per week. One is willing to pay $5 per week and the other is willing to pay $10 per week. One neighbor was also willing to pay an extra $25 for one week during the summer, to have your daughter "pet sit" for the week, meaning she visits once per day that week to feed, water and walk the dog.

This sample data might seem small, and it seems like it would easily be possible to sample the entire neighborhood to get exact data for the presentation, but the problem is that it is not realistic to sample your entire target consumer base when starting up your own business. You want to keep your daughter's sample area small to increase the likelihood that the actual business will not run quite as smoothly as it seemed it would on paper, because working through unforeseen problems is half the fun! Once all the data is collected, then it comes time to put it all together.

In our example, your daughter is going to present her business proposal on her laptop computer, so you will begin your next Weekly

Meeting by giving her a tutorial on the program you like to use on your computer (like PowerPoint), and how to use it. Then you'll explain that a business proposal has to be clear, direct and concise. Show her how to organize her ideas and her data into a few simple slides. Important points to consider are that she should use the same background pattern for all her slides and keep visual and sound effects to an absolute minimum; let the information speak for itself.

1. Her first slide should explain briefly who she is and what her work experience has been.

2. Her next slide will transition into what type of business she is trying to open.

3. Her third slide will be an outline of the income potential she assesses for her business based on her sample data. For example: based on my sample area of Main St from First St to Second St, (give data) I believe I will be able to charge $7 per week per dog, with an average of two customers per block. The boundaries of my business will be Main St. to Division St. and First St. to Third St., or about a four block area located in my neighborhood. Thus, I expect my weekly revenue to be approximately $52 per week.

Once she's established her income potential, it's time to move into expenses.

4. Her next slide will be titled expenses and list . . . yup, expenses. Start with weekly expenses. Weekly expenses might include:

- $15 per week in plastic bags to clean up after the dogs on the walks.

- $10 per week in dog treats to keep the dogs behaving appropriately.

5. The next slide will be start-up expenses and could look something like this:

    - Dog walking permit $150 (if the City does not require a permit I suggest you create a permit and charge her for it)

    - 5 retractable leashes: $75

    - 1 box of dog treats: $10

    - 1 box of plastic bags: $15

    - 1 Dog Clean-Up Tool: $30

6. The final slide will sum everything up for her audience: Based on my research in this area, this neighborhood really needs a Dog Walker.

    - Average weekly income = $52 per week with the potential to increase after my business begins to grow and gain publicity.

    - Estimated expenses = $25 per week.

    - Total start up costs = $280.

Disclaimer: if you were going to present your idea for a new type of nuclear reactor to the Department of Energy, you might not want to use a presentation with this simple a format, but keep your child in mind, here. This presentation will likely be the first time she has attempted to carve her own niche in the business world, so what you are trying to teach her are the basics regarding calculating income, expenses, presenting her ideas in a clear format and not forgetting that she has to abide by the laws that govern business practices in our society. If you are well seasoned in the area of running a business and you want to disregard this section and run it your own way, then more power to you. But implementing this section of The Family Bank and Financial System is important, because it brings together every aspect of our financial system in a concerted way, to give your child her first glimpse of the big picture and making her money actually work for her (aside from just earning interest).

Chapter 27

Presenting the Business Proposal

Once your daughter has her own LLC, has opened her business account, and her presentation is all ready to go and she has submitted her application for a business loan, the fun begins. The presentation of the Business Proposal should be the most fun and definitely the most

The Family Bank

entertaining section of The Family Bank and Family Financial System. In order for your daughter to get the start-up capital for her new business, she is going to have to approach a "venture capital" firm and attempt to get them to back her new Family Business. Not completely unlike being the CEO of The Family Bank, you are now going to play the role of CEO of the Family Venture Capital Firm.

When you determine that your daughter is ready to begin learning about entrepreneurship, then you will begin teaching her the basics in your Weekly Meetings. You'll want to ensure she understands that banks seldom give small business loans large enough to cover all of a new business' start-up expenses; therefore, she will have to approach potential financial backers or venture capital firms (possibly quite a few of them) to acquire the funding she will require to open her own business. You will cover all the semantics of how to get financial backing for her new business before she makes that initial appointment with you to present her idea.

Make sure she understands the process of walking into the venture capital firm in person to schedule an appointment to give her presentation, and, of course, let her practice giving her presentation to you in Weekly Meetings. Teach your daughter that she must be prepared and dressed for the part, in business attire at all stages of the process, including the initial walk-in to schedule the presentation appointment. She must always be ready, because she could possibly have to give the presentation on the spot during that initial walk-in, if the boss says she has time right then to hear it. Teach her to bring all her own electronics and other visual aids to both the initial request for an appointment and the final presentation at the venture capital office. Also, and I can't stress this enough, make sure she has plenty of time to practice her presentation with you before she even steps into your Family Bank Venture Capital office. Your daughter needs to be as prepared as possible and already know everything you have to teach her before she takes her first step into The Family Bank Venture Capital office.

During her preparatory run-up to her official presentation, you might walk through her slide show only once or maybe twice during a Weekly Meeting, but make sure you are as casual as you can be during the practice runs. You want her game day presentation to be stressful, so "dress up" for the dry runs in your pajamas and even feign disinterest; but give her a good, solid critique after each practice run and let her run through it as many times as she wants until she feels she has got it down.

Let your daughter come to you at your office, as the CEO of a venture capital firm, and schedule an appointment to present to you her business plan and request financial backing. You'll then give her a time and date to come back to your office and give you her presentation. You'll tell her she will have 30 minutes total for her presentation and to field any and all questions from you and your board regarding her new Family Business idea.

On the day of your daughter's official presentation, get dressed up as formal as you can muster, turn the lights on bright and bring all the family members you can find (also dressed in their most formal attire) to sit in the "board room" with you. When your daughter comes into your office for her meeting, allow for only a quick introduction, then pull out a watch and tell her you are really busy today and that she needs to keep the presentation to less than five minutes. Then sit back and watch her sweat while she madly clicks through her presentation, and try not to laugh. When she's done don't give her any real feedback or ask her any questions, just kick her out!

Practice Dinner—

A couple of days later, call your daughter back and tell her that you were really impressed with her business proposal and that you would like to get more information from her, but that you are very busy during the day. Let her suggest dinner and a date, time and location (this is important because she will be paying the real dinner bill).

You're going to have to cover setting up business dinners in a Weekly Meeting before you call her back, so that she knows what to ask for during the "call back" phone call and how to suggest a business dinner meeting. The best way to prepare her for the call back is by taking her to a practice dinner meeting, so she has some firsthand experience with the process of a dinner meeting and with the actual restaurant itself. So before the call back, take her to a nice restaurant; either to one of her choosing or one that you suggest, so she can get familiar with the people and the layout.

Introduce your daughter to the Maitre'D (usually the Manager or Head Waiter) and point out to her where the best tables are located. By meeting the Maitre'D ahead of time, she can ask for the table numbers of some of the better tables in the restaurant, so that when she calls the Maitre'D back later to make a reservation she can ask for the specific table number that she wants to reserve. Also, be sure to ask the Maitre'D during the dry run dinner how many days in advance your daughter will need to call in order to reserve a table; that way your daughter will know how many days out to schedule the dinner meeting during the "call back" phone call.

The business dinner is meant to be fun, but it is also meant to be a learning tool. Try to end up at the nicest restaurant your daughter can reasonably afford. You know what her accounts look like, so you be the judge. Truly nice, upscale restaurants have a different etiquette than your run-of-the-mill sit down place, so try to make it happen.

Dinnertime—

Dinner etiquette is complicated, so get yourself a copy of the *Complete Idiots Guide to Etiquette* or *Etiquette for Dummies* and go through it with your daughter during a Weekly Meeting. You can have her practice setting the table with the proper place settings and using the correct flatware for each course during normal family dinnertime. Explain that she still has to dress in business attire, although business casual suits (square-toed shoes, more than two buttons on the jacket, a colored dress shirt, and a color of suit other than black, navy or charcoal) are usually okay. Again, you'll go through your trusty etiquette guide, so she will know how to do the basics; placing her napkin in her lap to eat and left of her plate when she is done, which silverware goes with which food, how to hold her silverware and how much to tip.

Then hit the town. There is no better practice than the real deal, so go out and enjoy a nice dinner, but make sure your daughter is attentive to how the restaurant "flows" and how people look and behave. Ensure that your daughter has learned how to identify the Maitre'D, head waiter, servers and bussers, and that she knows how to tip. If her budget is too limited to go out to dinner, then set the dinner up at home. Set up a room to emulate a restaurant, with family members to help as the Maitre'D and wait staff, and make the dinner as formal as possible. Also, if you do the dinner meeting at home, be sure she is presented with the dinner bill. Taking a potential financial backer out on a business dinner is not the time to split the bill, so paying the bill herself is something that has to be done. Let your daughter know that sometimes, if a financial backer is seeking her out, that the backer might set up the dinner and pay the bill. All the better, but your daughter still needs to know the proper etiquette and make an attempt to pay the bill.

Don't forget, in all the excitement and preparation, that the dinner meeting is a time for you to truly dedicate an evening to listening to every idea your daughter has about her business plan. Chances are you are thinking she won't have more than ten words to say about it, but don't be surprised when she is still talking about her business two hours into the dinner; and remember, this dinner meeting is time for you to listen as a Venture Capital CEO, not to comment or critique her ideas as a parent or a Mentor.

Finally, this section could be an entire book in itself, but just make sure you get your basics covered. Like every section in this book, you can add volumes if you happen to be an expert in this area, but as long as you are covering the basics the best you know how, then you are giving your son or daughter an experience that no one else their age is even thinking about. If you were under the impression that a child's experience in business etiquette and formal dining depend primarily on the socioeconomic status of the family, you are mistaken. It doesn't. Even the richest people, who go out to expensive restaurants all the time, don't sit and teach their kids everything they know about how to get along in the business world and how to act at business dinners; and those who do, well, they will be successful, but they are few and far between and they will be your son's and daughter's colleagues and competition. One educational business dinner experience can, and will, introduce your child to a world that may have previously seemed unrealistic or unattainable. Your child can be a part of any society or any "world", even those that seem foreign to you, but it's up to you to "break that ice".

Chapter 28

Running The Family Business

This is simple. Reinforce every piece of information you have taught your daughter from age eight through today, and let her run her business the best way she sees fit. If she gets tired of it and "lets it go" after two months, with no ambition to start another business, then so be it. It's hers to do with as she pleases, as long as she pays back her financial backer and her small business loan! If she does give up on her business, then that's not to say that you failed or that you should have pushed her to keep it going. Her business is a learning experience and as long as she opened it and ran it for even a short period of time, the knowledge and experience she gained from it will stay with her forever. You never know, maybe fifteen years down the road she will be inspired by looking back on that memory and open up the next Microsoft or Google.

On the flip side, your daughter might open a Family Business that takes off and makes money hand over fist. Again, resist the urge to get involved in her business. Your only role is to advise her in the areas where she seeks you out, and to make sure that she is legally sound.

If she is making enough money that she has to file real income taxes, then you need to make sure the taxes are done correctly and that all her licenses and permits are in order. Teach her what you are doing while you are doing it, but take care of those items personally. This section is necessarily succinct, because every small business will be so different that the only parameter I give here is simply this: let her run it how she sees fit and deal with the problems that arise in the best way she knows how.

SECTION VIII

Life Long Financial Success

I'm sure you've noticed that I've been vague when it comes to many of the technicalities of running The Family Bank. For example, I told you to create a rental agreement, but I didn't tell you exactly what to put into it. The reason I've been purposefully vague when it comes to the particulars of your Family Bank is because no two families are exactly the same. The terms I put in my rental agreement will differ from yours and I don't want to steer you in the wrong direction or be unnecessarily restrictive. Also, the purpose of this book is not to create limitations, but to inspire you as a wise, knowledgeable and loving parent to create a Family Bank and run it however you see fit. I'm sure you already have a hundred ideas of what you will do with your Family Bank, so run with them. If you get to a technical portion of the Family Bank, like creating forms, and you don't know what to do, just search the Internet and improvise, using whatever you find. The Family Bank doesn't create any new economic theory or rewrite any textbooks, so everything you need can be found quickly on the Internet. Also, your Weekly Meetings are your own, just like your Family Bank forms and applications. Create what works best for your family, modify them as you see fit and allow them to evolve over time.

What are you willing to do for your kids? Are you willing to do anything? I'm guessing you would lay down your life for them, even if only to guarantee them a long, happy life. Fortunately, you can take a huge step toward giving your children everything you never had, at a far less dramatic cost. Just spend one Saturday morning creatively developing your own Family Bank and financial system, and then let it run. Think about it this way: you'll never have to hear your kids ask you for money or ask you to buy them something in a store ever again. If they want money from you, you wait until you get home and let them pick up a loan application from The Family Bank. No arguing. If they want to buy something from the store, they will buy it themselves and they will be the one to "hem and haw" over whether they really have the money to buy it, or not.

Now you have all the knowledge you need to get your Family Bank started!

Just to recap, you are teaching your kids everything they need to know about how to be financially successful as adults, but you're doing it one step at a time as they master each section of The Family Bank. You will be implementing The Family Bank over a period of many years, so don't feel like everything we discussed, especially the last half of this book, has to be (or even can be) implemented right away. Here is a reminder of what you need to do right away to get started:

- Get your journal and maybe a pocket calendar, a notebook for your child, a small dry erase board, a lock box, an in-and-out box and some scrap paper.

- Make a space in your house or apartment that is dedicated to The Family Bank and set it up. Remember it can be as small or as large as you want.

- Set up a time with your child for your first Weekly Meeting and to explain The Family Bank concept.

That's it.

Your kids will eventually thank you dearly for the lessons you instilled in them as they grew up, especially when they see their peers struggling with the stress and unhappiness that comes from overwhelming debt and poor finances. The Family Bank teaches your kids important lessons, and it does so in the safety of your own home; the important lessons that will help your children to become financially successful adults.

You will quickly fall in love with your Family Bank and the more proficient with it you become, the less and less work it will be for you. You will especially love those evenings, after you've posted a job for a dishwasher and hired your son, when you get to sit back and relax while he is loading and unloading the dishwasher after dinner, or cleaning your house!

If you are teetering on the edge and are not yet totally committed to starting your own Family Bank because, quite frankly, you don't know much about the business and financial world and you don't want to teach your kids any mistakes, then relax. Focus on just teaching them what you know and they will build on that knowledge in their own time and on their own terms. The Family Bank has taken all the real work out of teaching finances to your children by clearly organizing all the lessons and laying them out for you. All you have to do is run your Family Bank. So, if you are not yet committed to starting your own Family Bank because spending the time and energy to teach your children about the real world sounds like too much work, then I'm afraid I just can't help you, and no one will help your kids. Your kids will never be hurt by learning early on the lessons you struggled with to get where you are now . . . so get going, good luck, and don't forget to review all those journals with your son or daughter the day they turn eighteen and close those accounts.

That's it. That's the whole plan. Now go get started!

About the Author

Sergio Dinaro graduated with a Bachelor's of Science degree in Biology, with a minor in Biological Chemistry. Like so many of his fellow Americans, Sergio enlisted in the U.S. Army (as a Counterintelligence Agent) after September 11th, 2001, where he served his country dutifully in both Afghanistan and Iraq. After an honorable discharge from the Army, Sergio again found himself in the same boat as many Americans; an unemployed, financially unstable, college educated veteran, who was blazing through his life's savings.

Sergio took advantage of this "respite" from the work force to reflect on his life and his financial situation. He came to the realization that he was proud to have been able to serve his country during a time a great need; however, warm, fuzzy feelings were not paying the bills or putting food on the table. He was not at a place in his life where he could afford to be unemployed for any length of time. In short, Sergio found himself financially unstable.

Sergio set out to determine why he, raised in a typical American family, whose only desire as a child was to achieve the American dream, was struggling to make ends meet. Is it possible to grow up with very little, finance college, serve your country, enter the work force during a recession AND be able to pay your bills, buy a house and land the job you've always wanted? The answer he discovered was, "Yes!" Sergio looked at his 6 year old daughter and realized that he had unwittingly made too many financial mistakes early in his life, and that if he was going to teach his daughter how to be financially stable as she grows up, then he had to begin her education immediately . . . and The Family Bank was born.

CPSIA information can be obtained at www.ICGtesting.com
Printed in the USA
LVOW082203020812

292755LV00002B/46/P